After Lockdown

Bruno Latour

After Lockdown

A Metamorphosis

Translated by Julie Rose

polity

Originally published in French as *Où suis-je ? Leçons du confinement à l'usage des terrestres* © Editions La Découverte, Paris, 2021

This English edition © Polity Press, 2021

Cet ouvrage a bénéficié du soutien du Programme d'aide à la publication de l'Institut français / This book is supported by the Institut français.

INSTITUT FRANÇAIS

Polity Press
65 Bridge Street
Cambridge CB2 1UR, UK

Polity Press
101 Station Landing
Suite 300
Medford, MA 02155, USA

ISBN-13: 978-1-5095-5001-2
ISBN-13: 978-1-5095-5002-9 (paperback)

A catalogue record for this book is available from the British Library.

Library of Congress Control Number: 2021939921

Typeset in 11 on 14 pt Sabon by
Cheshire Typesetting Ltd, Cuddington, Cheshire
Printed and bound in Great Britain by CPI Group (UK) Ltd, Croydon

The publisher has used its best endeavours to ensure that the URLs for external websites referred to in this book are correct and active at the time of going to press. However, the publisher has no responsibility for the websites and can make no guarantee that a site will remain live or that the content is or will remain appropriate.

Every effort has been made to trace all copyright holders, but if any have been overlooked the publisher will be pleased to include any necessary credits in any subsequent reprint or edition.

For further information on Polity, visit our website: politybooks.com

For Lilo, son of Sarah and Robinson

Hast thou perceived the breadth of the earth?
declare if thou knowest it all.
Job 38:18

Contents

I

One way of becoming a termite

There are many ways to begin. For instance, like a hero in a novel who wakes up after fainting and, rubbing his eyes, looking haggard, murmurs, 'Where am I?' It's not easy, in fact, to tell where he is, especially now, after such a long lockdown, when he emerges into the street, face masked, to meet only the fleeting gaze of the few passersby.

The thing that especially disheartens him, no, alarms him, is that recently he has taken to gazing at the moon – it's been full since last night – as if it were the only thing he could still contemplate without feeling uneasy. The sun? Impossible to be glad of its heat without immediately thinking of global warming. The trees swaying in the wind? He's eaten up with the fear of seeing them dry out or go under the saw. Even with the water falling from the clouds, he has the unpleasant feeling he's somehow responsible for seeing that it arrives: 'You know very well it'll soon be in short supply everywhere!' Delight in contemplating a landscape? Don't even think about it – here we are, responsible for every kind of pollution affecting it, so if you [*vous*] can still marvel at golden wheatfields, that's because you've forgotten that all the poppies have disappeared thanks to the European Union's agricultural policies; where the Impressionists once painted swarms of beauties, all you can see now is the impact of the EU decisions that have turned the countrysides into deserts . . . No, really, he can only ease his anxieties by resting his eyes on the moon: for its circling, for its phases, at least, he in no way feels responsible; it's the last spectacle he has left. If its brightness moves you [*tu*] so much, that's because, well, you know you're innocent of its movement. As you once were when you looked at the fields, lakes, trees, rivers and mountains, the scenery, without giving a thought to the effect your every move might have, however slight. Before. Not that long ago.

When I wake up, I start to feel the torments suffered by the hero of Kafka's novella, *Metamorphosis*, who, while he's sleeping, turns into a black beetle, a crab or a cockroach. The next morning, he finds himself terrifyingly unable to get up to go to work like he used to do before; he hides under his bed; he hears his sister, his parents, his boss's lackey knocking on his bedroom door, which he's carefully locked shut; he can't get up anymore; his back is as hard as steel; he has to relearn how to control his legs and his claws, which are waving about in all directions; he gradually realises that no one can understand what he's saying anymore; his body has changed size; he feels himself turning into a 'monstrous insect'.

It's as if I, too, had undergone an actual metamorphosis in January 2020. I still remember how, before, I could move around innocently taking my body with me.

One way of becoming a termite

Now I feel like I have to make an effort and haul along at my back a long trail of CO_2 that won't let me buy a plane ticket and take off, and that now hampers my every movement, to the point where I hardly dare tap at my keyboard for fear of causing ice to melt somewhere far away. But it's been worse since January because, on top of that, I now project in front of me – they tell me non-stop – a cloud of aerosols whose fine droplets can spread tiny viruses in the lungs capable of killing my neighbours, who would suffocate in their beds, over-running the hospital services. In front as behind, there's a sort of carapace of consequences, every day more appalling, that I have to learn to drag around. If I force myself to keep the regulatory safe distances, breathing with difficulty through this surgical mask, I don't manage to crawl very far because as soon as I try to fill my trolly, the uneasiness intensifies: this cup of coffee is ruining a patch of the tropics; that tee-shirt is sending a child into poverty in Bangladesh; from the rare steak I was eating with relish emanate puffs of methane that are further accelerating the climate crisis. And so I groan, I tie myself in knots, terrified by this metamorphosis – will I finally wake from this nightmare, go back to what I was before: free, whole, mobile? An old-fashioned human being, in short! Locked-down, sure, but only for a few weeks; not for ever, that would be too horrible. Who wants to end up like Gregor Samsa, wasted away in a cupboard, to his parents' great relief?

And yet a metamorphosis there has certainly been, and it seems that we're not about to turn back by waking up out of this nightmare. Once locked-down, always locked-down. The 'monstrous insect' has to learn to move around lop-sided, to grapple with his neighbours, with his parents (maybe the Samsa family, too, will start mutating?), all hampered by their antennae, their vapour trails, their virus and gas exhausts, all jangling with their protheses, a hideous noise of steel fins banging together. 'Where the hell am I?': *elsewhere, in another time, someone else, a member of another human population.* How to get used to it? By groping around, feeling our way, as always – what else can we do?

Kafka hit the nail on the head: becoming a bug offers a pretty good starting point for me to learn to get my bearings and to now take stock. Insects everywhere are endangered, but ants and termites are still around. To see where it takes us, why wouldn't I start with their lines of flight?

The thing that is indeed nice and practical about mushroom-cultivating termites and the way they live in symbiosis with specialised fungi able to digest wood – the famous *Termitomyces* which turns the digested wood into a nutritional compost that the termites then eat – is that they build vast nests of chewed earth, inside which they maintain a sort of air-conditioning system. A clay Prague where every bit of food passes into the digestive tube of every termite in the space of a few days. The termite is confined, it's really a model of confinement, there's no case for saying: it never goes out! Except that *it* is the one who constructs the termite mound, drooling clump after clump. As a result, it can go *anywhere*, but only by extending its termite mound a bit further. The termite wraps itself in its mound, it rolls itself up in what is both its interior environment and its own way of having an exterior – its extended body, in a fashion; scientists would call it a second 'exoskeleton', on top of the first one, its carapace, its segments, and its articulated legs.

The adjective 'Kafkaesque' has a different meaning if I apply it to a lone termite, isolated without food in a prison-like world of dry brown clay, or if it instead refers to a Gregor Samsa, who is ultimately pretty pleased to have digested his mud home thanks to the wood snaffled up by his hundreds of millions of relatives and compatriots who've produced food that forms a continuous floodtide from which he has taken a few molecules in passing. This would amount to a new metamorphosis of the celebrated narrative in *Metamorphosis* – after many others. But then no one would find him monstrous anymore; no one would try and crush him as a cockroach in the manner of Daddy Samsa. Perhaps I should endow him with other feelings, exclaiming, as they did with Sisyphus, though for quite different reasons: 'We need to imagine Gregor Samsa happy . . .'

This becoming-an-insect, this becoming-a-termite could allay the terror of a person who now, to reassure himself, has only the moon to contemplate since the moon is the only close thing that's outside his worries. Since, well, if you [*tu*] feel such uneasiness looking at trees, the wind, rain, drought, sea, rivers – and, of course, butterflies and bees – because you feel responsible, yes, at bottom, guilty for not fighting the people who are destroying them; because you have insinuated yourself into their existence, you have crossed their paths; well, it's true: you [*tu*] too, *tu quoque* (you likewise); you digested them, modified them, transformed them; you turned them into your interior environment, your termitarium, your town, your Prague of stone and cement. But why then would you feel ill at ease?

One way of becoming a termite

Nothing is alien to you anymore; you're no longer alone; you quietly digest a few molecules of whatever reaches your intestines, after having passed through the metabolism of hundreds of millions of relatives, allies, compatriots and competitors. You're not in your old room now, Gregor, but you can go anywhere, so why would you continue to hide away in shame? You fled; now take the lead; show us!

With your antennae, your articulations, your emanations, your waste matter, your mandibles, your prostheses, you may *at last* be becoming a human being! And it's your parents, on the contrary, the people knocking on your door, anxious, horrified, and even your dear sister Grete, who have *become* inhuman, by rejecting becoming an insect *themselves*? *They* are the ones who ought to feel bad, *not you*. They are the ones who've metamorphosed, the ones the climate crisis and the pandemic have transformed into so many 'monsters'? We've read Kafka's novella the wrong way round. Put back on his six hairy legs, Gregor would at last walk straight and could teach us how to extricate ourselves from lockdown.

Since we've been talking, the moon has gone down; it is beyond your [*tes*] woes; alien but in a different way from before. You don't look convinced? The uneasiness is still there? That's because I reassured you a little too glibly. You feel even worse? You hate this metamorphosis? You want to go back to being an old-fashioned human being? You're right. Even if we became insects, we would still be *bad* insects, incapable of moving very far, shut away in our locked room.

It's this 'return to earth' business that's got my head in a spin. It's not fair to push us to come back down to earth if they don't tell us where to land so we don't crash, or what will happen to us, who we'll feel affiliated with or not. I was a bit too quick off the mark. That's the problem with starting with a crash site, I can no longer *position myself* with the aid of a GPS; I can no longer overfly anything. But this is also my chance: it's enough to start where one is, *ground zero*, and then try to follow the first track that crops up in the bush, and see where it takes us. No point hurrying, there's still a bit of time left to find a place to nest. Of course, I've lost my nice stentor's voice, the one that used to hold forth from on high addressing the whole human race, off-stage; like Gregor's to his parents' ears, my diction is in danger of sounding like mumbling, that's the whole problem with this becoming-animal. But what counts is to make heard the voices of those groping their way forward into the moonless night, hailing one another. Other compatriots may well manage to regroup around those calls.

2
Locked-down in a space that's still pretty vast

'Where am I?' sighs the person who wakes up to find they're an insect. *In a city* probably, like half my contemporaries. Consequently I find myself inside a sort of extended termite mound: an installation of outer walls, pathways, air-conditioning systems, food flows, cable networks, whose ramifications run beneath rural areas, for a very long way. The same way that termites' conduits help them get into the sturdiest beams of a house made of wood even over great distances. In the city, in a sense, I'm always 'at home' – at least for a minuscule stretch: I repainted that wall, I brought this table back from abroad, I accidentally flooded my neighbour's apartment, I paid the rent. Those are a few tiny traces added forever to the framework of Lutetian limestone, to the marks, wrinkles and riches of this place. If I consider the framework, for every stone I find an urbanite who made it; if I start with the urbanites, I'll find a trace of every one of their actions in the stone they've left behind – that big stain on the wall, still here twenty years later, is my doing, and so is this graffiti. What others take for a cold and anonymous framework, for me in any case virtually amounts to an artwork.

What goes for the city goes for the termite mound: habitat and inhabitants are in continuity; to define the one is to define the others; the city is the exoskeleton of its inhabitants, just as the inhabitants leave behind a habitat in their wake, when they go off or waste away, for instance when they're buried in the cemetery. A city-dweller lives in his city the way a hermit crab lives in its shell. 'So where am I?' *In*, and *through* and partly *thanks to* my shell. The proof of this is that I can't even take my provisions up to my place without using the lift that allows me to do so. An urbanite, then, is an insect 'with a lift' the way we say a spider is 'with a web'? The owners still have to have maintained the machinery. Behind the tenant, there is a prothesis; behind the pro-thesis, more owners and service agents. And so on. The inanimate framework and those who animate it – it's all one. A completely naked urbanite doesn't exist any-more than a termite outside its termite mound, a spider without its web or a forester whose forest has been destroyed. A termite mound without a termite is a heap of mud, like the ritzy quartiers, during the lockdown, when we'd idly amble past all these sumptuous build-ings without any inhabitants to enliven them.

If for an urbanite, then, the city is not exactly alien to his ways of being, can I actually go a bit further before I encounter something that really is *outside*? This summer in the Vercors region, at the foot of the Grand Veymont mountain, a geologist friend showed us how the entire top of this spectacular cliff was a graveyard of corals, another gigantic conurbation, long deserted by its inhabitants, whose remains, heaped, compressed, buried, then lifted up, eroded and suspended, had engendered this beautiful Urgonian chalk whose white stone with its fine crystals sparkled under his magnifying glass. He called these calcareous sediments 'bioclastic', which means 'made of all the debris of living things'. So there is no break, then, no discontinuity, when I go from the oh-so-bioclastic urban termite mound to this valley in the Vercors that a glacier once carved out of a cemetery of countless living things? As a result, I feel a bit less alienated; I can go on crawling along like a crab further and further. My door is no longer locked shut.

Especially as, climbing up towards the Grand Veymont, I'm reminded by the giant anthills punctuating our walk every hundred metres that they, too, lead the life of busy urbanites. Gregor must feel less alone, since his segmental body has been resonating with his stone Prague whose every aggregate of cristals preserves an echo of an ocean of shells clinking together. Enough to leave his family laid out on the tiles, imprisoned at home, in their poor human bodies *delineated* the old-fashioned way like figures made of wire.

When he was in his room, Gregor suffered from being a stranger among his nearest and dearest; a wall and bolts were enough to lock him securely in. Once he's an insect, he's suddenly able to *walk through walls*. From now on he sees his room, his house, as balls of clay, stone and rubble that he has partly digested then regurgitated and that no longer limit his movements. Now he can go out at leisure without being mocked. The city of Prague, its bridges, its churches, its palaces? – so many clumps of earth that are a bit bigger, a bit older, too, more sedimented, all of them artificial, manufactured things emanating from the mandibles of his innumerable compatriots. The thing that may well make becoming an insect bearable to me is that, going from the city to the country, I find myself faced with other termite mounds, mountains of limestone, every bit as artificial, bigger, older, even more sedimented by the long shrewd labour and engineering of innumerable animalcules. The confined deconfines himself perfectly well. He begins to rediscover enormous freedom of movement.

Let's follow this fine conduit, let's prolong this minuscule intuition, let's doggedly obey this bizarre injunction: if I can go from the termite mound to the city, then from the city to the mountain, is it possible to go to the very place in which I once had a hunch that all a mountain did was 'be located somewhere'?

For an ant, the work of the anthill forms a bubble around it while maintaining its temperature and purifying its air; and the same goes for Véronica, who heaves as she breathes, on the strenuous climb towards the Grand Veymont. The oxygen she inhales doesn't come from her, as if she had to lug on her back the heavy bottles the men who conquered Annapurna had to carry. Others, innumerable and hidden, invite her free of charge – for the moment – to fill her lungs with the stuff. As for the ozone layer that protects her from the sun – again, for the moment – it forms a dome above her that emerges from the labour of agents just as invisible, just as innumerable, and even older: two and a half billion years of bacteria in action. So, the puffs of CO_2 she releases in breathing don't make her an alien, a 'monstrous insect', but a breather among billions of breathers that some take advantage of to form the wood of the forest of beeches in whose shade she gets her breath back. Which makes this walker a pedestrian in an immense metropolis that she covered on foot one fine afternoon. Outside, here in the middle of nowhere, she is housed *inside* a conurbation that she can never leave without promptly dying of suffocation.

What a shock it is for Gregor to realise that manufacture, engineering, the freedom to invent, no, the obligation to invent, can also be found in what he took to be the air he breathed, the atmosphere, the blue sky, in the days when he was just a human reduced to a wire figure like his unworthy parents. For there to be a dome over his head, for him not to choke when he goes out – but that's just it, he doesn't really 'go out' anymore – what's needed are still more workers, still more animalcules, still more subtle arrangements, still more scattered efforts to hold the tent of the sky in place; one more long, immensely long, history of manufactures, just for there to be an *edge*, a vast canopy that's a bit stable and for him to survive in it for a while. If I want to swiftly learn from Gregor, the bug, how to conduct myself, I have to accept that it's through technical devices, factories, hangars, ports, laboratories that I'll best be able to grasp the work of living organisms and their capacity to change the living conditions around them, to build nests, spheres, surroundings, bubbles of conditioned air. It's through them that we can better understand the nature of 'nature'. Nature is not first and foremost 'green', it is not first and foremost 'organic'; it is above all composed of manufactures and manufacturers – provided we leave them the time.

It's strange that geology and biology manuals marvel that 'by chance' living organisms found the ideal conditions on earth in which they could develop for billions of years: the right temperature, the right distance from the sun, the right water, the right air. We might expect serious scientists to be less keen to embrace such a *providential* version of the harmony between organisms and their 'environment', as they say. The slightest experience of turning into an animal leads to a completely different view, one much more down-to-earth: there is no 'environment' at all. It's as if you [*vous*] were to congratulate an ant on how lucky it is to find itself in an anthill that's so providentially well heated, so pleasantly ventilated and so frequently cleaned of its waste materials! The ant would no doubt retort, if you knew how to question it, that it and billions of its congeners have emitted this 'environment' that emerges from them, just as the city of Prague emanates from its inhabitants. The idea of an environment scarcely makes any sense since you [*vous*] can never draw a boundary line that would distinguish an organism from what surrounds it. Strictly speaking, nothing surrounds us, everything conspires in our breathing. And the history of living beings is there to remind us that this earth that's so 'favourable' to their development has been *made* favourable by living beings to their designs – designs so well hidden that they themselves know nothing about them! Blindly, they have bent space around them; they have more or less folded, buried, rolled, balled themselves up in it.

Now I'm a bit better oriented, after all, because I'm beginning to get close to what is really 'outside'. In the tales of my childhood, when castaways washed up on a beach somewhere (like Cyrus Smith in Jules Verne's *The Mysterious Island*), they always raced to climb up onto some summit to check whether they happened to be on a continent or an island. Disappointed if it was an island, but reassured even so when it spread out before them, vast and diversified enough. We, too, realise that we're confined, certainly, but on an island that is still nice and sizeable and whose edge we can figure out *from the inside*, sort of against the light, as if we were in the middle of a Crystal Palace, a greenhouse, or the way a swimmer sees the sky when he looks up from underwater, at the bottom of a lake.

Of that outside – this is the most amazing thing – I long ago learned we never have a *direct* experience. Even the most daring cosmonaut won't repeat her spectacular space walks unless she's carefully squeezed into a tight *ad hoc* suit – a mini-sphere that connects her to Cape Kennedy as if by a solid cable anchored in the ground and which she can't quit without promptly perishing. As for the numerous testimonies about this vast exterior, about all that lies *beyond the threshold*, we read them, we learn them, we calculate them, but always *from the inside* of our laboratories, our telescopes or our institutions, without ever leaving these. Unless through imagination – or better still, through *illustrated* knowledge, via scientific inscriptions. As stirring as the view of our planet seen from Saturn is, it was inside a NASA office, in 2013, that the image was pieced together, one pixel at a time: to celebrate its objectivity, forgetting about the connections that let the earth be seen from a distance, is to misunderstand the object as well as the aptitudes of subjects to know with any certainty.

Crawling from room to city, from city to mountain, from mountain to atmosphere, sticking to the model offered by termites – the narrow conduit in which they make their way – I still don't know where we are, but I feel I can stick a stake in the ground so I don't get lost again next time I set out looking for locations. *This side of* the edge is the world which we have experience of and where we everywhere encounter various kinds of *compatriots*, who, through their engineering feats, their daring deeds, their freedoms, are able to build whole compounds that they organise in their fashion and that are more or less interconnected. The results of their inventions always surprise us, but we nonetheless feel that they share with our own people something like *a family resemblance. Beyond* the edge, it's a very different world, one that's surprising of course, but one we have no direct experience of except through the aid of illustrated knowledge; it will never be *familiar* to us. The outside, the real outside, begins where the moon revolves, this moon you [*tu*] were right to contemplate with envy as a symbol of innocence, alien, incorruptible in fact and, so, reassuring, understandably, for those who will always live in lockdown.

I'm looking for a name that clearly distinguishes inside from outside. It needs to operate like a great wall, a new *summa divisio*. I propose to call what's on this side *Earth* and what's beyond – why not? – the *Universe*. And those who live on this side, or rather those who *agree* to reside on this side, could be called the earthbound, or *terrestrials*. They're the ones I'm trying to enter into a relationship with in launching my calls. The names are provisional, all else being equal; I'm still only at the first sightings phase. But we already sense that Earth is experienced up close, even if we don't know much about it, whereas the Universe is often much better known but we don't have direct experience of it. It would be good if the rest of us, we terrestrials, prepared to don gear designed differently depending on whether we intend to travel on one side or on the other of this boundary, of this impassible *limes*. Otherwise, strictly speaking, we won't be able to grasp what enables the living to make the earth habitable; we *will make life impossible* for ourselves.

3
'Earth' is a proper noun

For the moment, the thing that's making life impossible for us is this *generational conflict* so perfectly described in the tale of Gregor Samsa. In a way, since lockdown, every one of us has been living through it in our own families.

In Kafka's novella, there is the family of wire figures on one side – the obese father, the asthmatic mother, the infantile sister – to whom must be added the tedious 'chief clerk', two young and horrified maids, the 'all-bones' charwoman and the three interfering lodgers. And then there's this Gregor whose transformation into an insect foreshadows our own. He is thicker now, heavier; he has more trouble walking, at least at first; his more numerous legs hamper him; his rigid back makes a dull sound when it hits the floor, but he can connect with many more things than they can – to say nothing of the fact that he can climb up to the ceiling ... And so, he feels more at ease, as there's nothing in his peregrinations as a creature who can pass through walls that doesn't remind him of his competence fairly freely to build nests, domes, bubbles, atmospheres, in short *interiors* that are not necessarily comfortable, but are always chosen by those who've formed them – engineers, urbanists, bacteria, mushrooms, forests, peasants, oceans, mountains or anthills – or, failing that, are organised by their forbears, often unintentionally, what's more. As for Gregor's parents, they're the ones who are walled up in their oversized apartment, whose rent they can't even pay. Inevitably, since the only interior they've got is the one drawn up in the eyes of others by the pretty cramped limit of their ugly bodies. They are still confined, whereas Gregor *no longer is*. As long as he hasn't reached the real exterior, the other side of the barrier, he remains inside a world that is pretty familiar, all things considered. For his parents, menacing exteriority begins at the door on the street; for the new Gregor, *interiority* stretches as far as the limits, admittedly still undetermined, of Earth.

The two generations, the one from before and the one from after the general lockdown, don't localise themselves the same way. To say that Gregor 'doesn't get along very well with his parents' is a euphemism: their ways of measuring things and his are well and truly incommensurable. They don't just lead to different quantities; their ways of registering distances simply have nothing to do with each other. It's not all that surprising that in the twentieth century, focused on issues to do with 'human relations', people saw Kafka's novella as a perfect illustration of 'communication breakdowns'. But they might have been wrong about the distance between Gregor's way of sizing himself up and his parents'. There is something literally crushing in the way the latter get their bearings in the world – that is, starting with a map.

We start with the Universe, come to the Milky Way, then the solar system, we reach various planets, before overflying the earth, then sliding on to GoogleEarth™ to get to Czechoslovakia, before reaching the space above Prague, over the neighbourhood, the street, and soon the dowdy old apartment block opposite the sinister hospital. At the end of this flyover, localisation of the Samsa parents is perhaps complete – especially if we add in the data from the land register, the post office, the police, the bank, plus, these days, the 'social networks'. But, in comparison with these vastnesses, Gregor's poor progenitors are reduced to nothing: a dot, less than a dot, a pixel blinking on a screen. The localisation is final in the sense that it *ends* by eliminating those it has located using mere latitude and longitude. The pixel has no neighbour, no predecessor or successor. It has become literally incomprehensible. Funny way of getting your bearings.

Having become an insect, and thereby a terrestrial, Gregor gets his bearings quite differently from the way his parents do. He is proportionate to the things he's digested and left in his wake, and when he moves around, a little clumsily to start with, it is always *step by step*. Nothing consequently can crush him by pinpointing him from on high and from a distance. In spite of old man Samsa's raised cane, no force can flatten him or reduce him to a pixel. For Gregor's parents, he is invisible and his speech is incomprehensible, which is why, in the end, they have to get rid of him ('it's lying there dead and done for!', the 'all-bones' charwoman announces with malicious glee). Whereas for Gregor, on the contrary, it's his parents who disappear, crushed and mute, if they're localised the old-fashioned way, cramped in their dining room as they are, reduced to their bodies, locked-down in their little selves, jabbering away in a language he can't stand hearing anymore. That is his line of flight.

If we follow Gregor's movement, we see that we distribute values in an entirely different way. We literally no longer live in the same world. They, the people from before lockdown, begin with their teeny little self; they add on a material framework which they say is 'artificial' or even 'inhuman' – Prague, factories, machines, 'modern life'; and then, thirdly, a bit further down the track, they pack in a whole jumble of inert things that stretch to infinity and which they don't really know what to do with anymore.

But we distribute our belongings altogether differently. We're beginning to realise that we don't have, that we'll never have, that no one has ever had *the experience of encountering 'inert things'*. That experience, supposedly common for previous generations, is something our generation, in a very short time, has gone through the ordeal of no longer sharing: everything we encounter, the mountains, the minerals, the air we breathe, the river we bathe in, the powdery humus in which we plant our lettuces, the viruses we seek to tame, the forest where we go looking for mushrooms, everything, even the blue sky, is the result, the product, yes we really must say it, the artificial result of agencies with which city-dwellers, every bit as much as country-dwellers, have something of a family resemblance.

On Earth, nothing is exactly 'natural' if we take that term to mean that which has not been touched by any living being: everything is raised, put together, imagined, maintained, invented, intricately linked by agencies

which, in a way, know what they want, or in any case
aim at a goal that is exclusively their own, each agency
for itself. There may well be 'inert things', forms that
unravel without a goal or a will. But to find them, we'd
need to go *to the other side*, up above towards the moon,
down below towards the centre of the globe, beyond the
limes, in this Universe that we can know but of which
we will never be able to have personal experience. We
know the Universe all the better, anyway, since it's made
up of things that gradually collapse according to laws
external to them, making their collapse *calculable* to the
tenth decimal. Whereas we always have a bit of trouble
calculating the agents that raise and maintain Earth,
since they persist, without obeying any law alien to
them, in going back up the slope that others only ever go
down. As they always go against the cascade of entropy,
with these agents you're always in for a surprise. 'Infralunar' and 'supra-lunar' weren't such bad terms, in the
end, for spotting the trace left by this great split.

It would be easy to say that your [*tes*] parents' generation sees death everywhere and that the following
generation sees 'life' everywhere; but the latter term
doesn't have the same meaning for both camps. Those
who consider themselves the only beings endowed with
consciousness in the middle of inert things, only count
as living beings themselves, their cats, their dogs, their
geraniums and maybe the park where they go to have a
stroll, once Gregor has been thrown out with the rub-
bish, at the end of the novella. Well, 'living', for you
[*toi*] who have undergone metamorphosis, doesn't just
describe termites, but *also* the termite mound, in the
sense that, without termites, this whole heap of mud
would not thus be laid-out and built up like a mountain

in the middle of a landscape (but the same goes for said mountain and said landscape . . .). Not to mention that, vice versa, termites couldn't live for a moment outside the termite mound, which is to their survival what the city is to city-dwellers.

I need a term that says that, on Earth, 'everything is made of life', if you understand by that the rigid body of the termite mound every bit as much as the agitated body of a termite, Charles Bridge every bit as much as the crowds swarming onto Charles Bridge, the fox fur every bit as much as the fox, the dam the beaver builds every bit as much as the beaver, the oxygen bacteria and plants give off every bit as much as the bacteria and plants themselves. Bioclastic? Biogenic? In any case *artificial* in the somewhat unusual sense that freedom and invention are always involved – hence the surprises at every turn. Not to mention the sedimentation that means that the termite mound, Charles Bridge, the fur, the dam and the oxygen hang on *a bit longer* than those from which they emanate – provided that other agencies, termites, builders, foxes, beavers or bacteria maintain their momentum. Unlike the generation that precedes us with their odd habits, we terrestrials have learned to use the adjective 'living' to refer to *both lists*, the one that starts with termite, and the one that starts with termite mound, without ever separating them. Which is something other peoples never forgot.

We can see how 'generational conflict' offers a bit more than a modern testimony to the incommunicability of human beings. I'm tempted to go further and say that it's really a conflict between geneses and, quite frankly, between *engenderings*. Because in the end it's not for nothing that terrestrials find a 'family resemblance' in everyone they meet. That is because they all have, or they all had in the past, what we might call *engendering concerns*. Those are after all, and movingly so, Gregor's immediate anxieties once he's become a bug: the thing that most upsets him is not seeing how he can meet the needs of his family!

I've just realised that the same thing goes for the ferns, spruces, beeches and lichens that try to withstand the harsh winters of the Vercors. But it was the same for the coral reefs that have since turned into this lovely Urgonian limestone that is the beautiful thing about the Grand Veymont, whose steep rock face dominates the celebrated Mont Aiguille. They all have to deal with issues of *subsistence* in the very simple sense that they must learn to stay alive. So I can understand how the engineers of the city of Prague are also keen to maintain Charles Bridge, jewel of the city, through regular inspections and numerous facelifts; how it is indeed the same kind of concerns that lead Baptiste Morizot to bring together wolves, sheep, dairy farmers, hunters and organic farmers around the ASPAS nature reserve in the Vercors; how it is indeed also through subtle inventions that the famous virus to whom we owe lockdown keeps on recombining so as to last a bit longer and spread further from mouth to mouth. What we can say of Earth is that it is the connection, association, overlapping, combination of all those who have subsistence and engendering concerns. An issue the Samsa family obviously simplified somewhat when Grete had the cruelty to ask: 'How do we get rid of it?' – speaking of her dear insect-brother . . .

I see, then, that I could explore this generational conflict more if I agreed to follow much further and, above all, *for a much longer time*, the lists of those who have engendering concerns. It actually turns out that it's in no way by chance that those agents always feel there's *a family resemblance* between them. That's because every existing being corresponds, step by step, to an invention, the specialists say a 'branch', that relates to a predecessor and to a successor; a small difference, that enables us to construct, again step by step, something like a genealogy, a family tree, often bushy, at times incomplete, that allows every one of us to go back, as they say, to their beginnings, just as a salmon goes back upriver, then upstream, then finally to the waterhole where it was born.

Urbanites have learnt to draw up their family trees; urbanists can tell you [*vous*], block by block, about the *evolution* – that's the word sometimes used – of their city. When they're in the country, a stone's throw from Saint-Agnan, geologists can do the same with the *history* – another word often used – of the sediments of the Vercors. And if you're lucky enough to walk around there with a botanist, he'll do the same for the sociology of the mountain plants that make the 'Strict Nature Reserve' at the foot of the Grand Veymont heavy with scent; and if Anne-Christine Taylor comes and joins you, she'll tell you instead about the cross-geneses of the wonderful Achuar gardens. The story will be more disturbing, more ancient, still more bushy, if you add a bacteriologist who reads Lynn Margulis to the walk, as he will take you to where the protists are and the archaea and introduce you to the feats of their combinations. But if you lose the thread of the story, you can always go back to more recent times with a visit to the excellent Musée de la Préhistoire (just below the Musée de la Résistance), in Vassieux-en-Vercors. This will allow you to follow other threads that connect the story of the silexes, pollens and silex cutters whose magnificent blades were exported to all of prehistoric Europe. You'll be amazed at each stage of these geneses, but you'll never lose sight of the fact that it's about solving problems that are, after all, familiar to you. Locked-down, yes, but *at home* . . .

Little by little, we see that the word 'Earth' doesn't refer to one planet among others according to the old positioning system, as if it were a name common to numerous celestial bodies. It's a *proper noun* that gathers together all existing beings. But that's just it: they are never gathered together into a whole – they have a family resemblance because they have a common origin and have spread, spilled over, mixed, overlapped, *just about everywhere*, transforming everything from top to bottom, incessantly repairing their initial conditions with their successive inventions. It turns out that every terrestrial recognises in his predecessors those who have created the conditions of liveability that he benefits from – Prague for the Samsa family, the anthill for the ant, the forest for the trees, the sea for the algae, their gardens for the Achuar – and that he expects to have to look after his successors. 'Just about everywhere' means *as far as* terrestrials have been able to extend and share their unique experience – but *no further*.

'Earth', then, is the term that comprises the agents – what biologists call 'living organisms' – *as well* as the effect of their actions, their *niche* if you like, all the traces they leave in passing, the external skeleton as well as the internal one, the termitaria as well as termites. Sébastien Dutreuil suggests we stick a capital on 'Life' to include living things and all they have transformed over the course of time, with the sea, mountains, soil and atmosphere included in a single line. If 'life' in small letters is a common noun that we hope to find just about everywhere in the Universe, 'Life' would be a proper noun designating *this* Earth and its so very particular organisation. But that would run the risk of introducing a new misunderstanding since the word 'living' is so much associated with the word 'organism'. Happily, to avoid confusing planet earth with a small e, common noun, and Earth with a big E, proper noun, I have up my sleeve a technical and scholarly noun, taken as so often from the Greek: Gaia, which happens also to be, for better or for worse, the name of a particularly fertile mythological figure. We won't say, then, that terrestrials are *on earth*, common noun, but that they are *with Earth* or *Gaia*, proper nouns.

4
'Earth' is feminine
– 'Universe' is masculine

I begin to position myself as a terrestrial among other terrestrials once the surprise has worn off and I realise that terrestrials never move around 'freely' everywhere in some undifferentiated space. They construct that space step by step. Curiously, it's feeling confined that gives us this freedom finally to move 'freely'. Turning into a termite assures us that we can't survive for a minute without constructing, by means of saliva and mud, a tiny tunnel that allows us to crawl in complete safety a few millimetres further along. No tunnel, no movement. We've lost the old freedom but only to gain another one. Gregor is finally able to move around, unlike his parents who are shut away at home, but for good. This obligation to pay for every movement by setting up a conduit liberates me as much as it does him: by snaking along, I'll be able to explore where I am for a bit longer – provided I pay the price.

The first thing is to see how far I can go and what the limits are of this new space I'm getting ready to stay locked-down in forever. By means of exploratory forays, it seems to me that terrestrials would pretty swiftly find their limits if they went *upwards* two or three kilometres or more – the exact distance is in dispute – or if they went *downwards* by two or three kilometres (an even vaguer measure), to where what geochemists nicely call the 'mother rocks' have not been fractured by any roots or by any running water, or degraded by any microbes. This would be the lower limit below which the Universe would start, in the depths of the planet. At least, that's what I learn by trailing around the corridors of the Institut de physique du globe in Paris, in the wake of Alexandra Arènes who is trying to delineate the new space. So this already gives us, us lot who are definitively confined, a pretty fair idea of our *confines*: terrestrials can move around, but only as far as the nappe, the biofilm, the current, the flow; the mounting tide of living things known as Earth or Gaia has managed to create somewhat sustainable liveability conditions for those that follow. Not a metre further than that foreshore.

If we need to learn to be happy with these limits, that's because we no longer wish to confuse the fine layer of life a few kilometres thick, which we can travel through with the appropriate equipment, and places we can't go to except through illustrated knowledge – whether we're talking about going to the confines of the cosmos or going down to the centre of the earth. Just as Gregor, having become a bug or a beetle, lies flat under his sofa to hide, terrestrials are realising that they need to take cover within a layer that's minuscule in comparison to what they once imagined of this outside world, which they chose to call the Universe and in which they previously had the impression they were travelling without constraint, finally locating each place thanks to the grid drawn up using the 'Cartesian coordinates' we learned in school by comparing scales on a map.

To designate this layer, this biofilm, this varnish, Jérôme Gaillardet has taught me to use the expression *critical zone*. It's fairly apposite, since understanding the zone's tension, fragility, edge, interface is, in fact, a *critical* issue. But we can't do so without changing the meaning of that particular adjective. When I was young, the previous generations understood 'critical spirit' to mean the capacity to learn to doubt by distancing oneself. Whereas living in a critical zone means learning *to carry on a bit longer*, without endangering the liveability of lifeforms that will come along after. The word 'critical' no longer refers just to a subjective, intellectual quality; it refers to a perilous and terribly objective situation, demonstrating *critical proximity*.

It's not just a question of space, but also of consistency in relationships, as if we'd changed worlds and nothing resonated as it did before. This is what gives people coming out of lockdown the feeling they've undergone the same metamorphosis as Gregor. At the end of the day, we're not exactly old-fashioned 'humans' anymore, and that's what makes us so uncomfortable, especially when we moan about these masks that half-suffocate us.

During lockdown, we, or at least the most privileged of us, found that even if we were not authorised to leave our apartments or walk further than the regulation one kilometre, we nevertheless had access, via 'communication tools', to *another world* of films, Zoom™, Skype™, and things like Netflix™. We were aware of a marked contrast between, on the one hand, the walls, furniture, bedroom, bed, cat, children that we could touch, measure, smell, and, on the other, the stories, courses, online purchases and *felines*, namely cats, that came from this other world but that we couldn't touch, or feel, or embrace. This allows me perhaps to point out that, relatively speaking, the same goes for the difference between the experience terrestrials have of their critical zone and the *indirect* understanding they may have of the Universe.

To access the latter, it's obviously not enough to have good wi-fi: you have to have access to streams of images, of inscriptions, traces, articles provided by instruments, sensors, probes, excavation campaigns, explorations, satellites, which have been invented over the course of time by vast communities of more or less generously funded scientists. And yet, as staggering as the series of data thus obtained are, as remarkable the imagination needed to interpret them, as precise the calculations that enable the data to be linked together, the fact remains that said scientists can't budge an inch from the office in which they gaze at the screens on which their data shimmers. They are all, to take up an expression the lockdown popularised, *working remotely*, meaning at a distance from the things they're talking about. They access these things as objectively as possible, but are themselves never dislocated. Besides, if they did stop consulting their screens, they'd be in danger of drifting from knowledge based on scientific inscriptions to the imagination, and then to the imaginary, perhaps even to reverie. However far they may go, if they want to know *for sure*, they have to remain riveted to their data, their noses literally in their calculations. Their view is thus never 'from out of nowhere'. This point deriving from the sociology of the sciences is something everybody got as they followed, day by day, the zigzagging progress of knowledge about the Covid-19 virus. No doubt about it, the slow and painful production of objective knowledge is added to the world, it doesn't overfly it.

It's vital not to forget this lesson of the lockdown, and incredibly dangerous to start confusing 'domestic chores' with working from home, because the behaviour of Earth's beings doesn't necessarily obey the same rules as the movement of things beyond the *limes*. While the things to which we have access in the Universe, through inscriptions, offer the spectacle, seen from incredibly far away, of *obeying* laws that are external to them, the engendering concerns of Earth's beings stem from the fact that their courses of action are *interrupted* every step of the way by the intrusion of the other actors on whom they depend. To confuse the two would be like a teacher thinking an online class could replace a face-to-face class; like a football fan confusing a video game with a 'contact' match; or like a philosopher taking the science done, readymade science, for science as it is done. Respecting this difference boils down to never losing sight of the countless *surprises* that arise and put paid to terrestrials' courses of action whenever they interact. (As an adjective, 'terrestrial' does not describe a type of existing beings – fleas, viruses, CEOs, lichens, engineers or farmers – but only a way of *positioning* ourselves as we run through the series of ascendants and descendants whose engendering concerns cross over for an instant.)

Online, we risk letting our heads go and thinking that phenomena merely *proceed continually* from an initial state to a predictable conclusion. We even go as far as believing that if we had the initial state, 'all the rest' would proceed 'as planned'. This is precisely the danger of a life of working remotely. With Earth, and, so, 'first-hand', it's all surprises at every stage. Continuity is necessarily the exception to the rule since engendering concerns demand that existing beings come up with something like an invention, a creation, however tiny, to achieve their goals by overcoming the inevitable hiatus in existence imposed by the multitudes through which those who want to carry on a bit longer have to pass. So it would be good if we didn't confuse access to the Universe *online* with life with Earth *on-site*!

Now, I feel strongly that previous generations – since what we're dealing with is indeed a generational conflict or, more precisely, an engendering conflict – have driven us to confuse the two kinds of movement. This is the sense in which they've made life impossible for us! Having tried for centuries to imagine the Universe based on the model provided by Earth – the famous analogy between micro- and macro-cosm – people then wanted to take a model of the Universe as an excellent way of remodelling life on Earth. Which boiled down to trying to *smooth over all hiatuses* so as to replace them with the simple *playing out* of phenomena known in advance and which supposedly *flow on* continuously from their causes to their consequences. Which boiled down to behaving as if there were no more engendering concerns to take into account to ensure continuity in any courses of action undertaken. And so what was once called, as ever in Greek, *phusis*, was sort of covered up, buried, concealed beneath 'Nature', which, as they used to say, quite rightly, in bygone days, 'loves to hide'!

What's more, it's on this distance between the laboratory and the field that researchers working on critical zones have built their paradigm: if the laboratory is so bad at predicting what happens in the field, this, they say, is because the phenomena that play out there rapidly are slowed down by the *intrusion* of thousands of other actors who come and add to the playing out of the desired chemical transformations by throwing their kinetics and complicating calculations. The more monitoring sites there are, the more Earth's *heterogeneity* increases. Well, to say a zone is 'heterogenous' is to insist yet again on those engendering concerns and on the mix of beings on which the zone's long-term liveability depends. Which means we really must invent *ad hoc* models that are more or less tailored to each phenomenon and virtually each site until all these tangles have been inventoried.

The thing that multiplies the difficulties is that Earth or Gaia has not spread 'everywhere'. I even saw, when Timothy Lenton started looking at the critical zone from the point of view of the Universe – and so from his office at the Global Institute of Exeter University, staffed by first-rate researchers who are as earthbound as they come – that Gaia weighed almost nothing – 0.14 per cent – compared to the energy coming from the sun, or compared to the energy fanning out from the centre of planet earth (a common noun which we no longer confuse with the proper noun). This explains the difficulty physicists have taking the influence of life seriously. Seen from afar, the biofilm in which terrestrials find themselves confined looks like a very thin lichen. Hence the temptation, which we must admit is very great, of totally discrediting what happens with Earth. A bit of dust, a bit of humus, a bit of mud. Poor terrestrials, having to pay for your subsistence second by second while patching up your pathetic DIY handiwork! Daddy Samsa's cane forever raised against these unfortunate bugs. As if life in face-to-face reality offered only a poor substitute for real virtual life.

But that doesn't stop Earth from being able, at times, to accommodate bits of the Universe. Luckily, by dint of calculations, and with a lot of gear and long apprenticeships, inside protected enclosures, we can actually create little reservoirs of the Universe in a vacuum, where things do proceed according to plan, flowing from causes to their consequences. This is after a host of exciting discoveries and long rehearsals in the course of which, naturally, nothing went according to plan ... Those reservoirs are the laboratories, so beloved by historians and sociologists of the sciences, the particle accelerators, the pile reactors, all the way up to the amazing ITER that manages, through a really extreme *lockdown,* to generate a few microseconds of fusion similar to the fusion that causes the sun to shine. Yes, but this feat occurs precisely at Saint-Paul-les-Durance, in the Bouches-du-Rhône, with the backing of many billions of dollars and, above all, without leaving an enclosure jealously guarded by technicians, engineers, inspectors and overseers, all perfectly terrestrial, under penalty of disaster.

These reservoirs, these puddles, these isolates of the Universe inside Earth, never form a continuous unit, except in dreams. It's more like a chain of *closed chambers* – oh, so very shut away! – each one of which depends on the ingenuity of living beings, engineers, researchers, technicians and managers. Nothing in these localities is able to *substitute for* the stuff Earth is made of. We all realised this, I think, when we saw the difficulties doctors and epidemiologists had day after day trying to 'standardise' what they knew about this bloody Covid-19.

Previous generations saw Gaia as weird splotches standing out against a homogenous, smooth and continuous space in the Universe. Terrestrials, on the contrary, are much more likely – reversing the image – to encounter on their travels little islands of the Universe maintained at great expense and standing out, through the sharpness of their edges, against the light cover formed by the chain link that tangled-up living things never stop mending. Yes, these archipelagos are wonderful; I have tears in my eyes every time I hear a beautiful experience described; but those are exceptions in a world that is continually supported by quite different agencies. As in those ambiguous images where the rabbit can turn into a duck and vice versa, what was in the background has shot to the fore.

So that's yet another apparently metaphysical story, for which the recent lockdown offers a truly wonderful model. We did in fact have to acknowledge, while we travelled online through 'infinite spaces' (or, failing that, were transported in multi-episode TV series), that we couldn't long survive without a whole host of jobs of which we had till then, we must admit, only a fairly vague awareness: catering jobs, deliverers, carriers, not to mention nurses, ambulance drivers and 'carers', a whole tribe of people as poorly paid as they were poorly viewed. Carrying out the simplest course of action like feeding yourself required the support of quite a few agents to 'ensure continuity' of the most ordinary life – we knew this vaguely but we confirmed it the hard way. The jobs that we tended to disregard became essential again, and the other way round. Suddenly, the work teachers do seemed pretty hard to parents called on to teach their toddlers sums or how to read. In every family, the great injustices in the division of chores between the sexes became more glaring. Daily life demanded constant work to ensure, here again, the simple repetition of days.

If the experience of lockdown seems to me so instructive, that's because it makes real the long history of the gradual elimination, over the course of time, of engendering concerns, which means you only have to look at the etymology of the word, concerns, or rather *gender troubles*. It's not for nothing that, in French anyway, Earth is a feminine (proper) noun – and how can we forget that the same goes for Gaia? – while Universe is a masculine noun. Along with other female philosophers and historians, Emilie Hache is reconstructing the strange divvying up that limits engendering issues to the procreation of females or mothers, imagining a quite different genesis for males, one that dispenses entirely with birth – or, in any case, has them be born later on *of themselves* and of *themselves alone* – autocthons! It's got to the point where people now identify women, birth, maternity and life, while males are supposedly born directly of the Universe – if only they'd accept being born . . . All engendering concerns are on one side, while the other half is freed from any concern about procreation, education or care.

It seems to me that terrestrials, as I've learned from Donna Haraway, like to tell themselves other stories, ones not much connected to those of their parents, *and especially not of their fathers*, and that they draw up quite different genealogies between themselves. We mustn't confuse engendering with identical reproduction. The last solution would be to *reduce* our capacities for geneses to only one of the two genders, as though the feminine had to be shut away in procreation, leaving the masculine . . . to what? Engendering can occur in many different ways – as Donna says, *'Make kin not babies'*. It really would be better to distinguish between those who acknowledge they were born, that they need care, that they have predecessors and successors – namely, terrestrials – from those who dream they were brought in by storks or came in cabbages, in any case that they emerged fully formed from the thighs of the Universe . . . and who wish only to go back there. These people, only a little while ago, still reserved for themselves the privilege of calling themselves 'humans'. So now they've had a shock that has disoriented them: Gaia and the feminine are not unrelated!

5

A whole cascade of engendering troubles

Things are panning out as if the lockdown imposed by the virus could serve as a model for familiarising us slowly with the general lockdown imposed by what is called, in a mild euphemism, the 'environmental crisis'. You [*tu*] know very well that it's not a crisis but a mutation: you no longer have the same body and you no longer move around in the same world as your parents. For the moment, what's happening to us is the same as what happened to Gregor, and we're terrified by this final shutdown. The strange promise implied by the title 'Metamorphosis', the term chosen in French (and English) as a translation of Kafka's *Die Verwandlung,* is not something you [*tu*] feel any more than I do – not yet, anyway. It's really too cruel not to be able to go on living like old-fashioned humans – meaning, modern humans. The strangest thing is that this anguish is shared by all, on all levels, about all existing things, to the point of introducing a sort of *universality of a new kind* completely foreign to what, not so long ago, used to go into the expression 'human beings'. It's as if we were seeing a whole cascade of troubles in engendering that might unite us, after all, by default.

The first place I find such anxieties is in political positions adopted. When young people baptise their movement 'Extinction Rebellion', you don't have to be a rocket scientist to see this as a symptom of agonising doubt about the flow-on of generations – and for them it's not just about the fate of human beings alone. You don't have to be a genius, either, to detect in the viral spread of themes to do with falling apart and collapse versions of the 'end of the world' so insightfully diagnosed by Deborah Danowski and Eduardo Viveiros de Castro. It's as if people were saying: 'There's no longer anything beyond this limit: *no future.*'

Am I wrong to discern a similar concern on the other side of the 'political spectrum', this time expressed by panic in the face of the return of the feminine, to the point where 'gender theories' are seen as an intolerable assault 'on the family' that obliges people to take up ever more stridently the 'fight against abortion' and the other forms of sexuality? How can we talk more directly about engendering concerns? And what can we say about this dread of the 'Great Replacement' (replacement theory) that the extreme right are obsessed with? Yes, of course, that's all about hatred of other human beings and not rage in the face of the destruction of non-human beings, but isn't it the same fear? At the very moment that opinions are believed to be more radically divided than ever, aren't they unified, after all, by the same anguish? If so, then a kind of broad threat of extinction is weighing on all political projects. As though the genealogical principle had suddenly been disrupted. Kafka would not have been surprised: 'political families', in fact, all have *family problems*.

The mutation shows up in the fact that politics no longer excites the same affections in us. Besides, during lockdown, we weren't worried about getting business up and running again swiftly, but quite the opposite, we felt wide-ranging suspicion about the interest of 'restarting' on the 'path of progress' and carrying on as before. Instead of immediately seeking 'recovery', it seems to me that a lot of us felt the risks run by the genesis of all forms of life. Suddenly the question the neighbours were all talking about was: 'What earth are we really going to be able to live on, my dependants and I?' How else can we make sense of these new forms of interest in the soil, in the land, in the local (not to mention the attraction of gardening and the strange passion for permaculture!) that would have seemed 'reactionary' to me ten years ago? If I can't easily place them between left and right, that's because everybody 'reacts' effectively in a thousand different ways to the same anxiety with a thousand different symptoms. As if the heart of public life was indeed well and truly occupied by the issue of *recovery*, only, the oh-so-very-existential recovery of generations – of insects and fish, climates and monsoons, languages and countries, every bit as much as human offspring. This is summed up pretty well, we must admit, by the figure of a return to earth, as if it were time to land for good – except that the earth we tried to take off from is no longer the same . . .

Doubt about being able to reproduce its liveability conditions is made even more painful by the breakdown of the 'international order'. As if we now had as much trouble defining the flow-on of our genealogical history as we do the limits of our national history. If there is an area of the old planet earth that in no way corresponds to the requirements, influences, mixes and relationships of the existing beings that form Earth, it would have to be the area defining the sovereignties we've inherited from the past. The reason for this, as Pierre Charbonnier so lucidly teaches us, is that every state delineated by its borders is obliged by definition *to lie* about what allows it to exist, since, if it's wealthy and developed, it has to expand over other territories on the quiet, though without seeing itself as being responsible for these territories in any way. That's a basic hypocrisy that creates a disconnect between, on one hand, *the world I live in*, as a *citizen* of a developed country, and, on the other, *the world I live off*, as a *consumer* of this same country. As if every wealthy state was coupled with a shadow state that never stopped haunting it, a sort of *Doppelgänger* that provides for it, on the one hand, but is devoured by it, on the other.

If a state was restricted to its borders, it couldn't live. Hence its anxiety: how to subsist? This awkward overhang is something we necessarily feel as anxiety, especially if we're wealthy; and even more so if we belong to the generations that have benefited from it the longest, the famous and so very cumbersome *baby boomers*. A suffocating feeling that gets worse as climate change intensifies. A panic that many of my fellow citizens seem to share in the form of an imaginary return to a past homeland, even more foreign to what would allow them to come back to life than the globalised world they were sailing towards till now. This only causes the temptation of nationalism to spread everywhere at the exact moment when that sweet term 'nation' no longer helps a people *to be reborn*. And yet it's all about renaissance, yes, but *where* and *who with*?

If we strongly sense that it's impossible for the citizens of nation-states, especially if those states are wealthy and powerful, to answer these questions, this is thanks to the very notion of a *border*, within whose shelter nation-states were supposed to protect their citizens but which prevents them, when all's said and done, from providing for them. Like the reserve in Kenya I visited with David Western, which a wealthy billionaire had surrounded with high fences so that his 'wild life' couldn't escape, but which, a few years later, had become a desert where only a few raw-boned cows grazed, too lazy or too weak to jump the wire fence. This is the new universal that is to be found wherever all existing beings live, but it's a particularly nasty universal: we're all affected by the *limits of the notion of a limit*; we find it hard to locate the *nomos* of the earth. It seems to me that the intrusion of Gaia is not only manifested in an interest in 'Nature', but in a general uncertainty about our protective envelopes. If lockdown is the bad news, the good news is the calling into question of notions of a border. On the one hand, we lose the strange idea of escaping beyond any limit, but on the other, we gain the freedom to move from one tangled mass to the next. On the one hand, freedom is frustrated by lockdown, on the other, we finally free ourselves of the infinite.

So, we need to stop thinking in terms of *identity* and start thinking in terms of *overlapping* and *encroachment* to come down a bit into the ethology of living things. Ecologists give the name *autotrophs* to those who feed themselves *by themselves* in taking up all they need to live on, extracting it from the sunlight after the fashion

42

of lovers who, as the saying goes, 'live on love and fresh air' (except that isn't true of lovers . . .). You [*vous*] could count bacteria and plants among autotrophs – and of course Gaia. In the strict sense, the legal sense, we could say that only autotrophs can rightly be considered autonomous, autochthonous and well and truly demarcated by a border. They alone have an identity. In the highly unlikely event that it would be of interest to them, autotrophs would benefit sort of naturally from an *exclusive right of ownership,* since they don't actually depend on any other terrestrial being to go about their business successfully. As for all the rest, the *heterotrophs,* all those we deal with on a daily basis, animals and people – they depend for their existence on a phantom body that is sometimes, like the states, of extravagant dimensions. And so they obviously have no right, no *natural right* anyway, to claim some exclusive privilege of ownership. Unless they are hypocrites and lie by denying the existence of the terrestrials that provide for them. Which is enough to trigger in every one of us, understandably, a huge moral dilemma. Our misfortune is to be confined but not to have a 'home', in the proper sense of the term. Yet it is precisely this that allows us to escape the traps of identity. Thanks to confinement, we can finally breathe!

If this demarcation between autotrophes and heterotrophs isn't completely clear, this is because bacteria and plants, inevitably, just through their metabolism, leave behind waste. A canonical narrative from the ancient history of the earth, what's more, has it that the cyanobacteria, utter autotrophs that they are, set about polluting the atmosphere two and a half billion years ago by expelling a form of oxygen that was highly toxic to their predecessors, those we call 'anaerobes', which, for this reason, had to take refuge in the depths to subsist. And so, even autotrophs have a decisive influence on the other terrestrials that have been forced to more or less manage with the unforeseen consequences of their actions. Emanuele Coccia likes to define even the 'higher' animals – humans included – as those that breathe the excreta of plants. That is actually a more precise definition of terrestrials: the way they depend on what provides for them *upstream* and get followers *downstream* to depend on what they expel. Earth is formed by concatenations like these.

This is where political affects are undergoing accelerated renewal, yes, a true metamorphosis. When 'humans' of the old kind present to other peoples as 'individuals' endowed with the privilege of exercising a right of exclusive ownership, they look more and more strange to us, we terrestrials. The right to be 'individual' can only be claimed by *perfectly autotrophic* living things *that leave no residue behind*. Which can only apply to Gaia, which, by definition, contains itself within its enclosures and in its niches. (According to the same logic, this would allow it to claim, if it was relevant to it, a proprietary right and even a fairly new form of sovereignty – watch this space.) But if there's one race that can never, in any circumstance or in any relationship, declare itself to be made up of individuals delineated much like wire figures, inside a secure border, that is indeed you [*tu*], the modern 'human', a race to which you once, not so long ago, were proud to belong. That, moreover, is why the description of Gregor's turning-into-an-insect seems so *realistic* in contrast to the novella's other roughly outlined characters.

A whole cascade of engendering troubles

The universal crisis that the lockdown has exposed is that all the legal and scientific tools which used to allow 'humans' to think about their relationships were applied to a world no one had ever inhabited! We can understand their terror. It was all about the setting of novels written by and about fictional individuals who are now suddenly realising that they live with Earth, forever entangled, ensnared, enmired, overlapping, in and on top of each other, without being able to limit these ties to either cooperation or competition. Yes, like Gregor, impeded by their legs and their antennae – to say nothing of their excreta.

The individual's limits were bursting at the seams, everyone was well aware of that. But now I understand why this figure that exists nowhere on Earth only found its most complete form very late in the day, in North America, after the Second World War, and, on top of that, in a novel as sloppily written as it was horribly effective, by a certain lunatic named Ayn Rand. Her story tells how, crushed, like Atlas, by the weight of the world they're holding up by paying too much tax, the entrepreneurs she admires decide to throw off their burden and take refuge in a mysterious valley, an imaginary second world invented so people could flee a world that was already imaginary – *Atlas Shrugged* is the title of one of this delightful person's novels! Only in this work of fiction, written in an 'offshore' land, do the heroes, individuals who are 'superior' because they 'don't owe anyone anything', decide to go on strike, starving all the poor wretches whom they've decided to deprive of their genial initiatives! As if Elon Musk's take-off for Mars was supposed to make the nine billion earthlings abandoned by him weep with sorrow

... *poor left-behind buggers*. With Earth, of course, we never meet any of these novelistic characters. In the real world, the individual is always a literary one-off, a *cogito* of theatre, as we've known ever since Descartes. And so, every time an individual presents himself as such and claims an exclusive right of ownership over some property, it ought to make us laugh.

The oddest thing is that what is true of the political individual is also true of the biological individual. If states are having some trouble 'managing', as they say, their resources as much as their waste, we mustn't hold that against them. Biologists have the same problem with what they call 'living organisms', whether these are complete animals or their cells or their genes. The cascade just goes on leaping further along in all the natural sciences in which we never cease gauging how hard it is to keep existing beings distinct from each other.

I've learnt from Scott Gilbert and Charlotte Brives that, paradoxically, if organisms really obeyed the constraints of neo-Darwinism, if they were really made of selfish genes, set in organisms that calculated their reproductive interests extremely exactly to the decimal point, they wouldn't be able to survive. Firstly, because they depend on niches that assure them more or less favourable liveability conditions, and, after that, because they need, at every point of their development, the unpredictable aid of other agents. What can natural selection of a cow mean if development of its intestine depends on the parallel selection of a myriad of bacteria that, however, are not part of its DNA? What is a 'human' body if the number of microbes needed for its maintenance exceeds by several orders of magnitude the number of its cells? Uncertainty over a body's exact edges is so great that

A whole cascade of engendering troubles

Lynn Margulis has suggested replacing the too narrow notion of an organism by what she calls 'holobionts'. Holobionts are a collection of actors in the form of clouds with blurred contours that allow somewhat durable membranes to subsist, thanks to the help the exterior contributes to what is held inside.

What makes lockdown both so painful and so tragically interesting is that the issue of engendering is now posed at all levels and for all existing beings, involving growing uncertainty about the notion of a limit. You've [*vous*] all realised that, even if we'll definitely see the end of it eventually, the Covid-19 pandemic merely foreshadows a new situation from which you will never emerge. Hence the eruption of a very paradoxical form of negative universality – no one knows how to extricate themselves permanently – which is positive at the same time – terrestrials see themselves as all being in the same boat. On the one hand, we feel like prisoners, on the other we feel liberated. On the one hand we're suffocating, on the other we can breathe. It's enough to make you wonder if the expression 'global awareness', which was pretty empty till now, hadn't started becoming meaningful. As if we heard in the distance this slogan, unexpected but more clearly articulated every day: 'Locked-down of the world unite! You have the same enemies, the people who'd like to escape to another planet!'

6
'Here below'
– except there is no up
above

What worries me the most when I try to share my thoughts about this fresh introduction of the global into politics is that I get the impression I'm depriving the people I talk to of air, as if I were cutting off the ventilator of a patient seriously affected by Covid. All the modern emotions drove us to extricate ourselves, to get out, to get free, to breathe deeply, and now suddenly, because of this mutation, we feel like we're suffocating. But then, after a while, we realise we're breathing easier.

The situation is all the harder for religious souls, who find themselves in limbo when it comes to expressing their faith. On the one hand, they only accepted living in this vale of tears *for a time* before being able to go off *elsewhere;* on the other hand, the feeling that the lockdown is definitive and that there's no question anymore of going off elsewhere or, applying a venerable metaphor, 'up to Heaven', finally gives the 'here below' its dignity, equally definitive. On the one hand, they feel like it spells abandonment of all their hopes; on the other, that it's finally the very condition for turning those hopes into reality. What meaning could they give the incarnation of a God made man if they had to get away out of this world?

Obviously, 'above' has never meant, as all believers know very well, an *altitude* that we could measure with a laser by moving through isotropic space – the space defined by the famous Cartesian coordinates. Believers who used once to direct their eyes, their hopes, their expectations 'up to Heaven', were not measuring a distance in kilometres, but a distance in *value*. The upper part of a Byzantine icon with its gilt mandorla is indeed 'on high', but that's to establish the greatest contrast with the 'here below' of poor sinners rendered in dark colours. Yes, that contrast tallies with what was later, when people believed themselves modern, to become the heavens, the *sky*. But in the end nothing in that particular sky – Heaven – means that we have really to go away by soaring off into the air for good (like the rocket that's meant to take the entrepreneur Elon Musk to Mars, to earthlings' great despair . . .). When the soul of the Blessed Virgin, gathered up by her Son, was taken to the top of the icon, it didn't rise stupidly through space, but was transmuted as it went *to Heaven*.

Except that everything has got more complicated since the old days, and in more ways than one. The gradual importation on Earth of forms of space travel imagined for the Universe has had the effect, since the seventeenth century, of making incomprehensible what was till now called the *here below*. That was an ancient, original, ancestral form of the terrestrial associated with the ancient *phusis:* a powerful feeling of confinement, of misery, of limit, of sickness and deaths to be mourned and lives to be taken care of. Which justified take-off to a beyond of peace, reward and salvation. The contrast between the high and the low was meaningful.

But, after that, the here below turned into 'matter'. Needless to say, there was nothing material about such 'matter', since all engendering concerns were evacuated from it on principle. That's what's so strange about the idea of an 'extended thing' – *res extensa* – to define the behaviour of the objects of this world; and the idea of setting opposite it a 'thinking thing' – *res cogitans* – is even stranger. It's clear that no one, despite all the efforts to extend this 'extended thing' everywhere, has ever lived by such a dichotomy, so contrary to experience. But as it nevertheless gave the impression of being able to travel anywhere without any renewed effort, this abstract idea of 'matter' had the effect of making it impossible to locate the Heaven towards which, in spite of everything, the hope of poor sinners still stretched. We went on looking up, but the sky had emptied. The Assumption of the unhappy Virgin no longer took place through a *transfer of value* towards Paradise in a deluge of golden hues and angels, but through a *translation* through space, with any number of *putti* and cumulonimbus. But that still didn't give this badly designed spacecraft the slightest aptitude to get moving for good.

The recurrent failure of these sorts of rocket launches fuelled the invention by believers, starting in the eighteenth century, of a 'spiritual' world, which they claimed to be able to locate still higher up than the up above, or at least very much above the 'material' world, and in which they could finally play at moving holy figures around at their leisure. It was in this higher 'spiritual world', placed like a bright horizontal layer *above* the darker layer of the 'material world', that the sequel to the 'after-life' story was supposed to unfold. An apparent end to confinement: finally a way out – at least for the dead, rolled up in their shrouds.

That invention would have been without great danger, would merely have covered the sanctuaries of churches with insipid frescoes and syrupy plaster statues, if the division between material and spiritual had not been *securalised*. Religious fervour can set off fits of madness, but securalised religion makes people mad for good. And that's what happened. In the flight from the 'material' world to the 'spiritual' world, the odour of opium distilled by the priests to lull the people was still too strong. But in the flight from the 'material' world to the apparently *rematerialised* 'spiritual' world, people could see nothing anymore but *positive* values, fit to fire up former sinners henceforth turned towards progress, the future, freedom, abundance, new figures for Heaven *amalgamated* with those for the heavens – the sky. They were aligned with the sky in that progress looked to be practical, realistic, empirical, but, of Heaven, these new figures preserved the decisive value, long borne by believers, of offering access to something final and absolute. This is known as having your cake and eating it. The amalgam was not of course stable but for a time it seemed irresistible: the same old quest for Paradise, but *on earth*!

Except that 'on earth', we feel this in sorrow, in no way means 'on Earth' – in the sense of being earthbound. By bringing back down an imaginary world that rose up, you've [*tu*] gone and fallen into an even more imaginary world. This is indeed where the effect of the lockdown makes itself most painfully felt and has everyone's head in a spin, even the most generous and the most idealistic. In fact, if the Moderns never stopped mocking the priests who lulled the masses with the promise of an imaginary 'next world' so that they *wouldn't act* in this material world here below, terrestrials, for their part, are in turn obliged to ridicule the Moderns, who lull the masses with their promise of an 'other world' that they have slowly come to realise – precisely thanks to the lockdown – is lulling them even more effectively by making it impossible for them to return to Earth – to touch down. Where the appeal of paradise prevented people from acting, the impossibility of realising paradise on earth has ended up paralysing all forms of action 'to get out'. The only thing that has been preserved is the ability to lull the masses, by spurring them on to smoke ever stronger doses of opium . . .

But *what* do we need 'to get out' of? Our paradoxical answer, the answer of the locked-down, of the earthbound, is that we need to get completely out of this not-so-material matter. But: to go where? For pity's sake! *To go back home, to the place where you are, the place you've never left.* The misunderstanding that caused the religious to wander off towards a spiritual world above the material one, and then the secularised religious towards a material world that supposedly had all the qualities of the spiritual one (except the religious!), arose from the fact that they confused the movement of things in the Universe with the engendering of living things with Earth. The famous 'extended thing', the *res extensa* of which the 'material' world was supposedly made up, has no palpable existence 'first-hand'. It's a handy tool for pinpointing on a grid something faraway, because it allows you to *sort* data into squares drawn up by Cartesian coordinates, but only by 'working remotely'. The hardwearing notion of 'matter' that supposedly makes up 'inert things' now looks like an amalgam between the telemonitoring of things that played out on the other side of the *limes* and the procedures used in description. As if we'd confused the map with the territory.

On the other hand, on this side, in the new here below, in the sublunar, we terrestrials never encounter 'matter' in the strict sense of the term, any more than we do 'inert things'. The only thing we sometimes do is disturb, reinforce, complicate the niches, bubbles, enclosures that other living things have, raise, maintain, envelope, superimpose, amalgamate with other living things – soil, sky, oceans and atmospheres included. In this sense, our experience of the world is not 'material'. It is not 'spiritual', either. It is *formed with* other bodies, to which we should add illustrated knowledge of remotenesses – but without our ever being able to go into orbit outside our homes.

Revisiting this story requires of us, it's true, the suppleness of contortionists: to get out of it, we need to get out of the idea of getting 'out', and so we need to decide to *stay* and even to *go out inside*! But this doesn't mean we're about to return, out of despair and for want of something better, to the narrow confines of the old material world (the old modern world), as if we were prisoners who'd resigned themselves to going back to their cells for want of being able to break out for good. Learning to pace up and down the critical zone doesn't mean either going backwards, or forwards to the here below of days gone by, or towards the material world that the Moderns wanted to make the most of while spurning it to escape elsewhere. We can't escape anymore, but we can inhabit the same place in a different way, and this means all acrobatics, as Anna Tsing would say, have now to be based on the new ways of *placing ourselves differently* in the same spot. Isn't that the best way, anyway, to sum up the experience of the lockdown? Everyone started to live *at home* but *in a different way*.

That's also the experience of terrestrials. When you [*tu*] look up at the sky, you no longer see divine head-quarters as your ancestors did, a consolation for their miserable lives here-below. And yet you don't see mere altitude there either, the altitude that measured its distance in kilometres as in the days when you believed you were modern. You're actually forced to see it as something like the *canopy* of an enclosure constantly held in place by the multifarious and multimillenial activity of billions of agencies. The limit of this atmosphere, for you, is no longer anything like the limit of a wooden beam measured by a ruler, which you could extend *ad infinitum* with another beam and another ruler; it looks like the *confines of an action* that has the same *kind of limit* as the external surface of an anthill in the eyes of an ant. It could be extended, yes, but definitely not by a ruler; only by the getting down to work, by the recruitment and upkeep of a new cohort of ants – and only if the conditions for such an expansion are favourable. The sky above terrestrials is not the same sky now as the one involved in the 'extended thing' of the past. It's a *membrane* that is actively held in place and that has to stay able to produce an inside and an outside. *Finiteness* doesn't have the same meaning for the wooden beam as it does for the anthill.

The argument has, alas, become familiar to us, we the confined, since we're living it on a day-to-day basis every time they tell us, as they did again yesterday, that the last ten years have been the hottest since climate records have been kept. This is actually where terrestrials feel most painfully that the difference between the supralunar and the infralunar, which they thought they'd been 'freed' of since Galileo, is well and truly back. We know very well that the bubble of conditioned air we reside inside depends on our own actions. This is the real confinement, this fate that we've collectively chosen for ourselves – without thinking.

Distressed by recurrent drought, we cry out: 'How the hell are we going to get out of this?' The answer is that *we won't get out of it,* not unless we agree to carry on our backs, like Atlas, the temperature, the atmosphere, the proliferating commensals which once looked to us to be a simple 'environment' that we didn't have to look after and 'in which' all we did was 'place ourselves' in the manner of a wooden beam. This is what becoming-an-insect is. This is metamorphosis. This is our new freedom, once we're freed from the old one, the one from before lockdown. You [*tu*] know perfectly well that there is no infinite exterior anymore, and when you look at the sky, from now on, you see an urgent job you need to carry out but that *you never stop putting off till tomorrow* (which explains why the spectacle of the moon soothes you so much today . . .). Balk all you [*vous*] like, you know very well that the burden that the entrepreneurs dreamed up by the sinister Ms Rand claimed to have thrown off is one you now have to lug on your back – though without being crushed by it.

For believers – but that's just it: it's no longer about 'believing' – everything now hinges on the ability to *live differently* in this same world that is no longer exactly 'material' in the modern sense. They're now released from the 'spiritual' and from the obligation to flee this world by turning their eyes to the sky. This is the chance Pope Francis is seizing for them: released from salvation in the form of a way out, they are hereby obliged to reinvest the value that religions depicted, a little naively and increasingly falsely, as 'on high' in contrast to the here below, and to do so thanks to other figures that work on the same contrast but shift it this time round to other images, other rituals, other prayers. No more high and low, no more material and spiritual, just the tension between life on earth and life *with* Earth? The same demand for finality and for the Absolute, but narrated in entirely different forms? This would allow us finally to understand, in fear and trepidation, what was latent in the figures of the past. Many people are trying their hand at this. It requires carefulness and tact, but it's essential that we have faith here, since the figure of the incarnation resonates with the figure of landing back on earth; or with the fact that the Greek word for 'limit' is *eschaton*, and so there are other figures of eschatology to delve into here – meaning, emblems for the *end*, for the *finality* as well as the *finiteness* of the world. 'Thou sendest forth thy spirit . . . and thou renewest the face of the earth' (Psalm 104:30). Without the Earth, what could Spirit possibly mean?

I've learned that we protected ourselves better from the toxic power of religions by going back to their original value rather than by secularising them. The latter always boils down to confusing the letter and the spirit, while losing the thread that ties values to the provisional figures that express them. We must not abandon the religions of salvation to their fate, because we terrestrials find ourselves up against an extreme version of religious religion and of secularised religion, which have merged 'God' and the 'Dollar', 'God' and 'Mammon', in an explicit project of definitive flight from this world that legitimises the destruction of the greatest possible number of resources, leaving the greatest number of supernumeries *left behind* to fend for themselves however they can. The end of the world – the end of their world – risks taking a terrifying turn in their hands. The mad desire to see the emergency exit of paradise-on-earth disappear can make movements that will do anything to escape lockdown dangerous. Climate-change denial may appear sinister, but it will soon look like a clever and almost benign version of the passions that risk being unleashed when we'll need to shake off the secularised religions that preach escape from this world.

7

Letting the economy
bob to the surface

Kafka told us how Gregor, having become an insect, had missed his train by only two hours when already his boss, hopping mad, and outraged at his employee's laziness, sent his 'chief clerk' to knock on the Samsas' door. Those locked-down by the pandemic experienced the same situation, only on a gigantic scale: in a few weeks, what was till then called the 'Economy', with a capital E, confused with what ordinary people called 'their world', suddenly ground to a halt. Suspendedness, suspension, suspense. Every one of us sensed that through this 'world standstill', a flaw had been introduced into the claim to irreversibly define the action of all human beings, and that we could no longer confuse the Economy, the fabulous magnification of certain calculations, with the scholarly disciplines of accounting and economics – in lower-case – practised by often highly respectable calculators. Like Gregor, encumbered by his legs, every inhabitant of the planet found themselves standing there with their arms dangling: what to do? In the humblest hovel there was a sort of radical reversal of values: the top sank to the bottom, the bottom rose to the top.

A revolution, if you like, but of a very particular kind. As if the Economy, seen till now as the indisputable bedrock of existence, *rose to the top again*, in the manner of a wooden beam, kept artificially underwater and suddenly left to float to the surface. Without a shot being fired, the legendary 'infrastructure' of modern life appeared *superficial*. And, parallel to this, through an unhoped-for substitution, what the know-alls had hitherto seen as a completely negligible 'superstructure' slid under, slipped down into the depths: *engendering concerns* and *subsistence* issues. In a few months, the Economy stopped being the 'insuperable horizon of our time' (as Sartre said of Marxism).

Hence the racket made at all the doors of all the locked-down by scandalised 'chief clerks' to get people 'back to work' and 'speed up the recovery'. But in the chaos that ensued, and even through the global crisis that is unfolding right under our noses, we sense that their hearts aren't in it anymore, and that all the 'chief clerks' in the world can't get the masses to forget that, for a brief moment, they'd clearly seen the superficiality of that way of looking at things. This time round, it's not just a matter of improving, changing, greening or revolutionising the 'economic' system, but of *completely doing without the Economy*. By a paradox that never stops delighting terrestrials' hearts, it's the episode of the pandemic that has had the effect of *freeing* the minds of the locked-down and allowing them to emerge for a moment from this long imprisonment in the 'iron cage' of the 'laws of economics' in which they were rotting away. If ever there were a case of liberating yourself from the wrong liberation, this is definitely it.

I learned this from Michel Callon: belief in the obvious fact of this mode of relationship can only spread by transporting lifeforms to a world they did not reside in. That's always the difference between living 'on-site' and having access 'online'. The strange thing about the Economy in fact is that, being concerned with the things that are the most ordinary, the most important, the closest to our everyday preoccupations, it nonetheless insists on treating these as if nothing could be more remote, and as if they proceeded *without us*, captured by Sirius and in the most disinterested way – 'scientific' is the adjective sometimes used. That works beyond the *limes*, but not this side of them. *Homo oeconomicus* has nothing native, natural or autochthonous about him, as we've long known. Strictly speaking, he comes from on high, yes, *from the top down*, and not at all from ordinary, practical experience, *from the ground up*, from the relationships that lifeforms maintain with other lifeforms. The Economy only looks like a lever if we agree to import the modes of behaving of things so as to simplify the engendering mode of terrestrials.

For the Economy to expand and be kept down in the depths as the bedrock of all possible life on earth, an enormous work of infrastructure-building is required to impose it as obvious fact against the dogged resistance put up by the most common experience in reaction to such violent colonisation. The Economy may well end up acting 'in depth', but only in the manner of those enormous cement pillars that have to be driven into the ground by being battered by giant pile drivers so they can serve as a foundation. Donald MacKenzie has never stopped exploring this: without the schools of commerce, without accountants, lawyers, Excel tables, without the endless labour of states aimed at divvying up jobs between public and private sectors, without the novels of Ms Rand, without our being continually broken in by the invention of new algorithms, without the standardisation of property rights, without the continual drum-beating of the media, no one would ever have invented 'individuals' capable of a selfishness drastic enough, constant enough, consistent enough to not 'owe anyone anything' and to see all others as 'aliens' and all life forms as 'resources'. Beneath the evidence of a native, primal Economy lie three centuries of economisation, as Callon would put it. We can see how this preliminary embedding requires extreme violence and how the slightest pause in this vast support enterprise produces an immediate revelation: 'But why wouldn't we start with where we live, instead?' The thing that terrifies the 'chief clerks' is that, in quitting the Economy, terrestrials are merely going home and returning to ordinary experience. You shouldn't have left us hanging for so many months, only to plunge us afterwards into a global crisis that just keeps getting bigger.

Freed by lockdown from this interplanetary translocation, terrestrials have retrieved the right to once again see that engendering concerns never cease to complicate courses of action. We're all rediscovering that every agency on which we used to count adds a hiatus, forces a detour, complicates a sum, opens a debate, involves a scrupule, requires an invention, imposes a new distribution of values. And that these are the kinds of concerns we need to devote ourselves to. The issue is not whether the 'world of tomorrow' will replace the 'world of before', but whether the surface world couldn't finally give up its seat for the world of ordinary depth.

How do we go about making sure that this depth, for which the locked-down have developed a taste, isn't lost? The question matters because we are all, for the moment, like prisoners released on parole who risk going back inside their cells if they muck up again. I'm indebted to Dusan Kazik for the answer to how not to re-offend. It consists in *never agreeing* to say of any subject whatever that 'it has an economic dimension'! Bowing to that dimension, in fact, always boils down to suggesting that, on the one hand, there is a profound, essential, vital reality – the economic situation – but that, on the other hand, we could nonetheless, if we had the time, take 'other dimensions' into account – social, moral, political dimensions, and even, why not, if there's anything left over, an 'ecological' dimension . . . Well, reasoning accordingly means giving the mirage of the Economy a material reality it doesn't have, and lending a hand to a power that trickles down from on high. The Economy is like a veil thrown over various practices to hide all the hiatuses in courses of action. Like Nature, it, too, likes to hide . . .

Kazik's solution consists in always replacing any invocation of an 'economic dimension' with another question: 'Why have you decided *to divide up* life-forms *that way to* resolve your engendering concerns?' When the FNSEA (Fédération nationale des syndicats d'exploitants agricoles), the French farmers' union, lays siege to the Ministry so that it will re-authorise the use of bee-killing pesticides in order, they say, 'to save the French beet-sugar industry', we should not necessarily see this as having an 'economic dimension', if what we mean by that phrase is a calculation of indisputable interests that ought automatically to save forty thousand jobs and so many billions of euros. There has been a prior *distribution* of lifeforms, each one of which merits questioning: why save this industry, why grow beet sugar, why sugar, why these particular jobs, why the EU subsidies, why do the beekeepers and poppies have to pay the price for them, why does the state have to go back on its decision to ban neonicotinoids, what's the role played by aphids compared to the role played by drought, and so on? If there's one temptation we absolutely must not yield to it is *to smooth over all these hiatuses* so as to replace them with some sum that would close the discussion, a sum that has been *done elsewhere, by others* and especially *for others* far from the scene. This doesn't mean we hate beet sugar or that we should starve beet growers, and it may even be that it would be preferable, at the end of the discussion, to authorise said applications of muck for want of an alternative, but it does indicate that there is nothing in this web of discussions, negotiations, assessments that we should *by default reduce to the Economy* – and thereby to the superficial aspects of the case. Inevitably there is something *deeper* in the situation that we're going to have to take into account. On this side of the *limes*, nothing is smooth. We need to force ourselves to lift the veil every time.

This doesn't amount to whingeing until we get other preoccupations put above the Economy, concerns that are supposedly 'more noble', 'more human', 'more moral' or 'more social'. Quite the opposite: it means really taking stock of the fact that it's high time we delved *further down*, by becoming more realistic, more pragmatic, more materialistic. We don't live in the Nature invented by the economists so as to have their sums circulating freely in it. If we're rightly scandalised that religions invented the 'spiritual world' so as to have their holy figures circulating in it, we should be even more shocked that people have invented an 'ideal material world' just for the convenience of moving algorithms around in it – a bit like retired railwaymen, mad keen on model railways, who get trains circulating in their clubs using reduced-scale models, but don't carry a single passenger. Economists are of course justified in expanding their tool kit so as to *open* these discussions, but not one of their tools can claim to *close* them. Dusan is right: it's not about making a fresh attack on economics; it's about *abandoning* it altogether as a description of the relationships that lifeforms maintain with each other. The Economy casts its spell, but we need to learn to exorcise it.

It all seems easier when we realise that the ability of the Economy to play a role as infrastructure depends on the parallel introduced very early on in the piece with the working of 'nature and its laws'. It's this parallel in fact that sparked the idea of assimilating the laws of the Economy with the laws of 'Nature' and of making it play this astonishing infrastructure role. Well, if there's one trap that we terrestrials are not about to fall into it's the trap of thinking that 'Nature' designates a realm that lies on Earth! This is where Gaia intrudes, making a serious dent in all our habits of mind. We can invoke wolves all we like (wolves being, as we all know, wolves for man), bees (who contribute to the common good through their legendary selfishness), organs (which sacrifice themselves for each other), ants (always hard-working), sheep (sheep-like), viruses (which have to be wiped out), bugs (which horrify the Samsa family), and of course termites, lambs, eagles and piglets – you will never get terrestrials to believe that these imaginary behaviours could serve them as a model for establishing relationships with those they depend on. For the simple reason that these entities are not autotrophs, that their activities never cease spilling over, slobbering on, overlapping each other, merging with others to the point of making precise calculations of self-interest impossible.

No living thing can serve as an emblem for the calculating individual that Earth nowhere harbours. All living things are, if you like, selfish and self-interested, since they're all trying to go on living, but none of them fits snugly into clear enough limits to be able to calculate its interests *without getting it wrong*. If we really want to call on terrestrial agents to justify locking humans up in the 'iron cage' of the Economy, then we should be prepared to see that cage overflowing with sources of error, while piling up causes of disorder on top of other causes of disorder – in short, to expect countless complications. Calling on living things has never allowed us to simplify any situation whatever. That is where the 'appeal to Nature' is as far as it can possibly be from introducing Gaia. Accepting the experience of lockdown means finally being freed from the limits of an indisputable identity. Genes may well wish to be selfish, they still need to have a *self* they can delineate.

They tried hard to force through the parallel between Nature and the experience of life on earth, but to do so they had to yet again *secularise* a religious idea: the idea of a providential order of Creation. The idea of a process of calculable and consistent natural selection allowed some to hold on to the sacred notion of an 'order of nature' that put every living thing in the exact place its calculations of self-interest justified. It was only by inventing a providential vision of Nature in which 'beasts' would fight tooth and nail in the jungle of life that people were able to see humans 'as beasts'. Except that the 'beasts' actually had plenty of other worries – as did the jungle! What's known as 'Social Darwinism' did indeed have the goal of slotting the discoveries made by the naturalists into the sublime ordering involved in 'the economy of nature', but that remained at bottom a religious idea and not in the least earthly. If poor humans have such a lot of trouble calculating their interests selfishly, despite their accounting apparatuses, imagine how it is for bacteria, lichens, trees, whales or azaleas. Holobionts don't have bank accounts.

Certain evolutionists have since shown that if living things had calculated perfectly accurately, they would never have managed to survive. This doesn't mean that we have to swing from competition to cooperation. It simply means that it is miscalculations that end up creating, randomly and without the slightest hint of a providence, conditions of liveability that other living things, downstream, have seized on, the way the famous oxygen-producing bacteria have, unintentionally, enabled other organisms to try new solutions; or the way deforestation in southern China opened up 'great opportunities', as we know, for Covid-19. Step by step, for hundreds of millions of years, these miscalculations are what has enabled the engineering of more and more robust conditions for resisting the growing radiance of the sun, as well as ice ages, meteorites and volcanoes, without ever trying. So many enclosures, spheres, membranes, domes whose durability depends on their superpositions, their concatenations. Provided that the introduction of one particular extraterrestrial is strenuously avoided: the ideally selfish individual, that meteorite of a specific kind who really taxes the resilience of this whole vast makeshift job. If there are processes that do not enable the 'founding' of the Economy, they are indeed the processes borrowed from the means Gaia adopts to persist in being. 'Nature' can only serve as an indisputable foundation to extraterrestrials.

That's what allows us to get our bearings pretty well, nevertheless, even if negatively: we terrestrials *have never inhabited* the house of the Economy. The Samsa family will just have to get used to it: Gregor will not resume his place as a sales representative so he can bring home the bacon. Daddy Samsa can raise his cane all he likes and the 'chief clerk' remind Gregor, bug that he is, that he'd be better off getting up and going to work if he doesn't want to be fired, Gregor will refuse to budge. We can never simplify our relationships by assuming that there are individuals with clearly demarcated edges, lined up alongside each other, *partes extra partes*, autonomous and autochthonous, and who could declare themselves quits in relation to each other, strangers as a result, *aliens* in a way, as if they didn't live on top of each other, as if they didn't interact with each other. Let's celebrate the experience of a pandemic that has made us realise, as literally as this one has by making us keep our distance of a metre and forcing us to wear masks, to what extent the distinct individual was an illusion.

Let's make what the lockdown has revealed bear fruit: since we no longer have to transport ourselves to some ultra-world, we can start looking again at *where* we will live here-below. Obviously what we gain on one hand we lose on the other, since we can no longer calculate relationships from afar by taking cover from their consequences. But the game is worth the candle if we've taken what we can no longer calculate and learned to *describe* it together and above all *up close*.

8
Describing a territory – only, the right way round

During lockdown, it was inevitable that every one of us began reflecting on what could possibly replace the Economy, suspended as it was for a time. Hence the questions we asked ourselves: why continue this or that activity; why not come up with something different; what do we do with those whose livelihoods depended on the activities we'd like to stop; how do we develop businesses we think are beneficial, and so on? Those of us at least who had the leisure to do so, felt free to invent a different material base for themselves. At first, it was like a game to make use of the pause, then it got more and more serious, as if we were actually going to be able to stop everything from going back to what it was 'before' – even if we didn't really believe it.

The funny thing is that, by dint of imagining the 'world after', the locked-down gradually got the impression they were living *somewhere* and not just *anywhere* anymore. Actually, they never used to attach much importance beforehand to such issues of *subsistence*, or, in any case, these seemed to be decided elsewhere, by others and especially for others. To our eyes, they formed a sort of ineluctable necessity, shadowy obvious fact, and so gave us the impression that we didn't live anywhere in particular – something that was covered precisely by the all-purpose term, 'globalisation'. But little by little, thanks to your [*vous*] confronting such inhabitual questions and especially to realising that it was extremely hard to answer them, you were forced to wake up out of a dream and ask yourselves: 'So where the hell did I live *before*?' Well, in the Economy, actually, meaning *somewhere other than at home*.

Conversely, every time you had trouble answering those questions, you felt yourself *situated*. You were pinned to the spot as if by a series of reference points. The obligation to stay locked-down at home took on a positive sense: shut away, yes, but *grounded* somewhere at last. Even stranger, this feeling of being forced to situate yourself ever more precisely only intensified as you discussed these questions with others. The expression 'living in a globalised world' suddenly sounded seriously old-hat and was swiftly replaced by another injunction: 'Let's try and situate ourselves in a spot we'll need to try and describe in tandem with others'. Surprising association of verbs: *to subsist, to make a group, to be on a particular patch of soil, to describe oneself*. For the former globalised, it was a total shock to see the reemergence of the old 'reactionary' option of forming a group on a territory that became visible as it was being described. 'Territory', that administrative word, took on an existential meaning for the locked-down. As if, instead of being drawn up remotely by others and sort of the wrong way round and from on high, it was something we could describe for ourselves, along with our neighbours, the right way round and from *below*.

Describing a territory the wrong way round and from above, as we know, means consulting a map, locating a point at the intersection of abscissae and ordinates; after that it means writing down symbols, at these intersections, to replace the places to be pinpointed by their simple relationships in terms of distance in kilometres. The operation is nice and handy when you need to briefly visit a place you don't know in advance. Provided of course that the road departments have done their job and taken care that the map visitors hold in their hands coincides with the signs stuck in the ground at the spot marked by a chain of surveyors – all under the supervision of engineers from the Department of Civil Engineering and other decentralised government departments. For map and sign to coincide, a well-run state has to organise their correspondence. Then, and only then, will the map inform in advance about the territory, enabling a stranger to travel through it.

This is not, of course, the way we'd go about describing *our* territory, even if we say hello politely to passing strangers and avoid knocking over the theodolites of the engineer-surveyors. For us, distances in kilometres and angles of trigonometry, as all geographers know, are relationships among many others. Well, these other relationships in no way proceed by *tracking* based on a grid of coordinates, but by *answers to questions about interdependence*. What do I depend on to subsist; what are the threats that weigh on that which provides for me; what confidence can I have in those who tell me about those threats; what do I do to protect myself against them; what are the aids I might find to help me extricate myself; who are the opponents I have to try to contain? These questions, too, draw up a territory, but the drawing produced doesn't tally with the previous manner of getting our bearings. Being tracked is not the same thing as *situating oneself*; in both cases, what is measured is indeed *what counts*, but it doesn't count in the same way. Gregor and his parents learned that to their cost.

While, seen from the wrong way round, a territory is whatever can be located on a map by drawing a circle around it, seen the right way round, a territory will extend *as far* as the list of interactions with those we depend on – but no further. 'For where your treasure is, there will your heart be also' (Matthew 6:21). The first definition is cartographic and more often than not administrative or legal: 'Tell me *who* you are and I'll tell you what your territory is.' But the second is more ethological. 'Tell me *what* you live off and I'll tell you how far your living arena extends.' The first requires an *identity* card, the second a list of *affiliations*. Project the territory of a migratory bird on to a map of the world and, as Vinciane Despret has shown, you won't understand much about what makes it sing. Everything changes if you start to find out what it eats, why it migrates, how many other living things it needs to rely on and what dangers it has to confront along its paths. Its living arena will spill over the simple map projection on all sides.

On the one hand, we identify a place by locating it at the intersection of coordinates through the movements of a sort of chain of surveyors; on the other, we learn to list *attachments* to entities that force us to take care of them. With the wrong-way-round territory, we favour access to strangers who merely pass through a space that is for them undifferentiated; in the right-way-round territory, we enter into step-by-step contact with *dependants* who slip in, in ever greater numbers, between us and our engendering concerns. Wrong-way-round, what counts are measurements in terms of distance, but at the same time, we're perfectly free to stop there or elsewhere; nothing prevents us from arbitrarily taking up a different map or driving round as if we had a a GPS, *ad infinitum*. Whereas, the right way round, it's not initially distances that count for you [*vous*], since the entities that enter into your description can be remote or close on the map.

On the other hand, you can't possibly go on to infinity for the very good reason that the list of entities is always limited, is hard to draw up and demands a sort of investigation every time, the beginnings of a confrontation, in any case delicate encounters. You can't extend the list or shorten it arbitrarily: if you've had trouble entering these lifeforms on it, that's because they barge in on your description and *commit* you to taking them into consideration. You can make the list longer, of course, but then you'd have to *revisit* the description and commit *further* to confronting those you've listed – which will inevitably cause the tension to mount as your exploration goes deeper. This is what Isabelle Stengers calls *obligations*: the more precise your description becomes, the more it obligates you. Coming down to earth doesn't mean going local – in the sense of the usual metrics. It means being able to encounter the beings we depend on, *however far away* they may be in kilometres.

That's the whole misunderstanding of the adjective 'local' in a nutshell. It's only if you survey a situation the wrong way round that you'll define that situation as 'local', meaning by this that it's 'small' in relation to another one that would measure more in amounts. A map actually only recognises linked scales, which is what allows us to do Zoom meetings. But once it's put back the right way round, we call 'local' *what is discussed and argued in common*. 'Near' doesn't mean 'a few kilometres away', but 'what attacks me or provides for me *in a direct way*'; it's a measure of *commitment* and *intensity*. 'Distant' doesn't mean 'far away in kilometres', but whatever you don't have to worry about straightaway because it has no *involvement* in the things you depend on. Consequently, what you bring together in your description is neither local nor global, but *put together* according to a different relationship of concatenation with entities you're going to have to confront one by one, maybe at the cost of countless polemics.

That is furthermore the reason why a planisphere or a terrestrial globe gives no idea of Gaia since it's not 'big' or 'global' in the usual senses, but connected step by step. Both senses of the word 'local' or of the word 'remote' may sometimes coincide, but it's not very likely. These days, the world *we live in* only rarely overlaps with the world *we live off*. It's been a long while since the inhabitants of industrial societies lived in the middle of pasturelands, like Boaz asleep (in Victor Hugo's poem) when 'Ur and Jerimadeth were all at rest' . . .

As soon as you describe a territory the right way round, you feel in your bones why the Economy could not be realistic and materialistic. This is because it's made to hide the clashes, tensions and controversies that your description, conversely, no longer seeks to avoid. Embracing the Economy means interrupting the resumption of interactions by inventing beings who won't have to account for themselves on the pretext that they're autonomous individuals whose limits are protected by an exclusive right of ownership. A right that only applies to autotrophs that leave no waste behind downstream. As these particular animals don't exist on Earth, we can understand how deeply perplexed the pause imposed by Covid-19 made the hapless economised. They've realised that the limits of the right of ownership only managed to freeze situations that would heat up and become burning hot as soon as the descriptions were lengthened by several people.

For instance, my neighbour, who is a great lover of maize – or, more exactly, a great user of EU subsidies for irrigated maize – invades the bodies of my grandchildren with his herbicides. If I tell him to respect my ownership right and *to keep to himself* and see that his herbicides are confined within the limits of his fields, he will retort, more or less politely, that he's 'feeding the planet' and that 'he doesn't have to *account* for his actions to me'. If I reply that I have the same right as he does not to be invaded by his pesticides, any more than my lawn ought to be grazed on by his straying sheep, or that his children be bitten by my dog, he will probably tell me that we're in the country, and that *no one can carry out his activities* without *interfering* with those of others. Contrary to the nonetheless extremely bucolic proverb, 'Good fences make good neighbours', he will protest that he can't shut anything up inside closed boundaries: the cock-a-doodle-doo of the cock spills over village space just like pesticides, church bells, the dog, cattle and the milk spilled on the ground by Perrette (in La Fontaine's fable) – surely during the course of the nth demonstration against the government . . . and that that's what living in the country is all about.

'Ah, very well,' I'll say, 'so, *you acknowledge it yourself*, we live together on territory where "*everything is our business*", since each entity overlaps with the others. "Holobionts of the world unite, etc." But then, if we live tangled up like this, we really need to talk about it! If we spill over each other like this, then we form a *common*. So, please tell me the place, the time, the day, the institution, the formula, the procedure that will let us discuss these overlaps, limit encroachments or allow arrangements that are fairer for all?' He'll most likely blow his stack or try and stomp on me as if I were another Gregor.

All the same, his refusal allows me to measure exactly what the Economy is doing when it *disguises a situation*. It replaces a contradictory collective description that might have taken shape if the protagonists of this invented conversation had formed *a people living on a soil*, and if we had therefore been able to take into account in common the overlapping of these lifeforms. Describing ties of interdependence forces us to start again, for each item on the list, the discussion that the Economy aimed to close.

If there is overlapping and encroachment, then there must be something like a public problem and, so, a form of institution capable of revisiting the issue of the distribution of lifeforms that are inexorably interlocked. Strictly speaking, the Economy depopulates and throws people off the land. What lockdown allowed us to do was to *repopulate* and *resituate* those who agree to be judged on their ability to maintain, or on the contrary to destroy, the liveability conditions of their dependants.

Describing a territory – only, the right way round

Terrestrials would be welcome to label as 'ecology' not a domain, fresh focus on 'green stuff', but simply what the Economy turns into when its description *restarts*. If the one extended everywhere, the other should too. If the one cooled down the planet before leaving it to burn, the other should warm up its ties so it cools down at last.

Such institutions don't exist? Very well, at least we now know *where to situate ourselves:* terrestrials have recovered from the crash of the Economy, and they are settling in to build these institutions as if they were in the charred frame of a huge airship. To start with, let each and every one of us make contact with his neighbour again. Description repositions, it repopulates, but also, and this is the most unexpected thing, it gives you back a taste for action. We're beginning to go from an admittedly fairly hopeless 'mutation' to a more promising 'metamorphosis'. Yes, we're suffocating behind our masks, it's true, but we may well finally be about to take 'another form'.

9
The unfreezing of the landscape

This change of form hinges on a simple observation: we human beings have never had the experience of encountering these 'inert things' that, it seems, made up the 'material' world. This is obvious if you live in the city, since every millimetre of your living environment has been made by human beings, your fellows; but it's also obvious if you live in the country, since every detail of your territory is the work of a living thing – sometimes far removed in time. And this sensation of the consistency of things is true as far the critical zone extends. 'Inert things' only exist in a thought experiment that transports you [*vous*], in imagination, into a world no one has ever lived in. Hence the question: does the sensation of this obvious fact now modify your ways of being, of envisioning the future, of situating yourself in space, of understanding what you call freedom of movement?

To explore the possibility of such a transformation, it would be good to have a device that could convey these ever more concrete descriptions of the territory as seen from below. With Soheil Hajmirbaba, we tried to do this by drawing a large circle on the ground, oriented by an arrow, with a sign saying *more* on one side and a sign saying *less* on the other. Then we asked the participants to stand in the centre. Behind you, on the right hand, there's what you depend on, what provides for you, what enables you to subsist; on the left hand, what threatens you. In the front right-hand quarter, there's what you'll do to maintain or improve the liveability conditions you've enjoyed; in the front left-hand quarter, what threatens to worsen the situation, by sterilising a bit more the living conditions of those who depend on you. It's like a children's game, light-hearted and a lot of fun. And yet, when you get near the middle, everyone gets a bit nervous: you have to make up your mind, and that's the hardest thing, you reveal yourself; you're going to talk about yourself or, better still, about what keeps you alive.

The centre of the crucible, where I timidly put my feet, is the exact intersection of a trajectory – and I'm not in the habit of thinking of myself as a *vector* of a trajectory – which goes from the past, all that I've benefited from so as to exist, to grow, sometimes without even realising it, on which I unconsciously count and which may well stop with me, through my fault, which won't go towards the future anymore, because of all that threatens my conditions of existence, of which I was also unaware. It's hardly surprising if I'm moved. Oh, yes, it's extremely naive, it's incredibly simplistic: it's like choosing between good and evil. But that's exactly the point: it's a judgement that you pass in tandem with the others helping you play this game of hopscotch by answering questions about what keeps you alive, then about what threatens you, and, lastly, about what you are doing or not doing to counter that threat. Nothing could be simpler, nothing more decisive. Ah, right, so that's why the drawing looks like a target, and you're the one who finds themselves in the bulls-eye, on the line dividing the past and the future. This is where you have to make the leap: *Hic est saltus*, as Aesop would say. In every sense of the word, you're *replaying your life*.

That's just it, every time you're about to name out loud one of the entities on your list, someone in the gathering comes 'to play' that 'role', and it's up to you to place this character on this sort of compass – or to move them around as your short narrative evolves. The amazing result of this little enactment is that you're soon surrounded by a small assembly, which nonetheless represents your most personal situation, in front of the other participants. The more attachments you list, the more clearly you are defined. The more precise the description, the more the stage fills up! Little by little, you're giving shape to one of these holobionts that seemed, till now, so hard to represent. A woman in the group sums it up in one phrase: 'I'm repopulated!'

How can we mark such a mutation? By saying that terrestrials never find themselves *facing* a landscape anymore. In describing your interdependencies, for the others and through the others, it's as if the ground rose up under your feet and knocked you over. Territory is not what you occupy. It's what defines you. We can see that the metamorphosis works the other way round: it's Gregor who now seems almost 'normal' and his parents whose position seems incredibly contrived. They thought they were free and that he was a prisoner of his mutant body, but it's the reverse that happens.

Figures 1a and 1b. La Mégisserie, Saint-Junien, 1 February
2020. Launch of the 'Où attérir ?' ateliers.
Photography: Nicolas Laureau.

The unfreezing of the landscape

As art history has long explored, old-fashioned humans, modern humans, were strange in that they were fixed in place, almost pinned in a box with a wall at the back that was like a painting – this is the *white cube* of museums, the white cube of art critics. On this painting were represented all sorts of things that had suddenly been *stopped* in their movement, in their trajectory, so that they held still under the gaze of the spectator – or, more precisely, the person who was about to *become* a spectator, thanks to being required to judge the quality of the painting.

Such a weird scenography! You ask a perfectly decent bloke to stop what he's doing and come in off the street, you spin him round ninety degrees, you shut him up in a box and ask him to stand still, all contorted, so he can look at the form things take on this vertical board. But those entities, too, have been interrupted in their course of action and also been spun round ninety degrees. They're no longer being asked to prolong their existence, but to submit to the gaze of the spectator, offering him, if we can put it this way, their best profile. A lot of fuss has been made about the spectator's gaze, but the contortions forced on him are nothing beside those imposed on the agencies forced to interrupt their trajectories so they can be gazed at.

At the back of the back wall, if we agree to paint 'in perspective', the things interrupted distribute themselves according to size so as to provide the illusion of a space in three dimensions. In front of the wall, the neo-spectator gets down to judging the quality of the painting by noting, as he pleases, what seems to him appropriate or not, up to the point of producing another illusion: the illusion of a valuer capable of a disinterested aesthetic judgement. The tableau, the territory, ends up flattened as if wedged between two pyramids, one whose apex is virtual, a bit like the famous *vanishing line* that continues to infinity; the other, whose tip is in the eye of the beholder, who now has only to look.

If he has before him a landscape, say, with a mountain, a lake, a sunset, a herd of deer and, in the left-hand corner, a forest, it's up to him, and to him alone, to decide if the sun is 'well rendered', if the lake couldn't be 'lighter', the deer 'a bit more spread out', while the darkness of the forest is, again in his view, 'magnificently evoked'. It's the spectator who judges and who decides, to the point where every relationship between forest, sun, lake, animal and sky goes *via him* and is established for *his sole good*. It scarcely matters, moreover, whether what's been stuck in front of him is an old master, an industrial development project, a battle plan, a view of the sky, a theatre scene or the map of a realm some prince hopes to control. As Frédérique Aït-Touati tells us, it's always whatever is 'facing', a *landscape*, that seventeenth-century European invention. The subject (for he is now a 'subject') doesn't leave the white cube, from which emerges a vision in the form of a landscape, with, obviously, on the other side, things rendered in object mode (for these are now 'objects') which are, in a way, tailored to him. This is the great scene reconstructed by Philippe Descola: the person who remains fixed in this box will become a *naturalist* subject facing *naturalised* objects. That's what's so odd about this story: 'Nature' only exists for a subject. And he will remain confined to this box. Both he and the things are pinned like butterflies in an entomological drawer

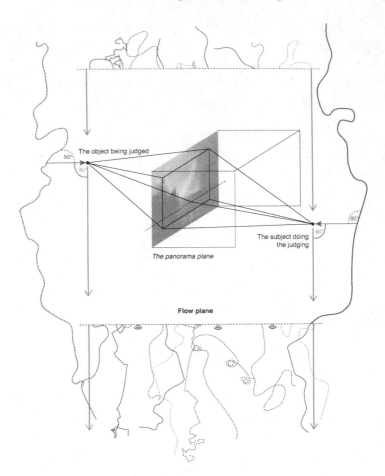

Figure 2. Drawing by Alexandra Arènes

by two fine needles, with these inscriptions written in black ink on labels with blue edging: 'modern object', 'modern subject'.

Yet another paradoxical result of the lockdown: it is from just such a box that it has allowed us to extract ourselves! The title 'metamorphosis' should be read the other way round: it's Gregor who takes an animated form again and his parents who are stuck in the impossible position of remaining subjects fixed in front of objects that are themselves fixed.

What happens if the protagonists of this scene set out again, spin round ninety degrees once more, but this time in the right direction, and get back into the flow of things that will also take up their course again and stop letting themselves be represented only by others? On the side of the 'objects', there will be a joyous stampede. The forest, lake, mountain, deer, ground are still there, but they *no longer go via* the subject in order to decide what suits them or not: they go on their way again by deciding *by* and *for themselves* what will allow them to carry on a bit longer. Here again, here once more, it's like the thawing of a river. End of naturalism.

But the 'subject' doesn't remain shut away either. Of course, at first, he's a bit stiff, he lacks exercise, but he'll swiftly get his suppleness back. Repopulated, the person starts running in the same movement as the lifeforms, pressed by them, jostled by them, grabbing the ones he depends on, sideways, on the fly, and deciding, on the spot, in the moment, the fate of those that depend on his actions. It's as if, instead of standing on the footpath outside your place watching a demonstration go past in front of you [*vous*], you decided to join in. A spectator till that moment, you're now forced to go in the same direction as the noisily worked-up crowd, sharing the same engendering concerns with every one of the entities on your list. You no longer see the things 'facing' you, it's true, but unlike the old 'subject' put in front of the old 'objects', you're no longer outside their dynamics. End of anthropocentrism.

We'll always be able to paint a picture, but the orientation of the image and the sampling mode won't be the same. We'll no longer ask beings who've set out in motion again to suspend their course, any more than we ask fish to smile politely for the camera capturing their spawning in a fish ladder. It'll be more like making *cuts* in an image-stream, using sensors to spot the vivid passage of all these tangled trajectories. Yes, in this painting, the deer moved, the sun set, the forest was lopped: yes, in this other one, there are now fences, trees have been replanted, there are cows and their calves, the sky is rainy; but what gets recorded this way is not the passage of time by the clock, but the freeze-frames of the decisions made by living things so they can continue being.

And *among these lifeforms* – and this makes all the difference – there are side roads that this repopulated person must take, using a compass, because from now on, in this crowd, in this stream, in this demonstration, just like the others he must decide his own fate. Did he defend the forest against logging, authorise the fences, promote the replanting, maintain the water quality of the lake? Is it instead the deer who made off, the larches that weren't able to withstand climate change, the lake that the drought lowered? The same questions apply *in parallel* to all lifeforms that flee or flow with each other, come together and part. Not *vanishing* lines stretching to infinity anymore, but *life lines* – what Chantal, as a musician, would call *fugues* (a fugue, in French, meaning running away from home, as well as the musical form).

The repopulated person finds himself grappling with the situation. Which means that he has a right to *redis-*

cover ascendants and descendants. The territory he reconstitutes bit by bit no longer belongs to him, he is *judged by it.* Sarah Vanuxem would say that the territory has become – or rather again become – its owner. This is the *nomos* of the earth. The metamorphosis has taken place: the participant has gone from being the 'subject' who faced a landscape and turned into the *vector* of a decision to be made between ascendants and descendants. And *between the two*, at this intersection, in this crucible, he will be judged by his capacity to decide on the *fecundity* or *sterility* of lifeforms with which his fate is now entwined. He finds himself hopping around in a game of hopscotch where his fate will be decided, between Earth or Heaven.

This is where the word 'metamorphosis' starts to fulfil its promise, provided we read the novella the other way round. To localise an individual, we're bound to add a context to him that crushes him and in relation to which he is almost nothing. The break between him and the context is total. This is the usual sense of the adjective 'Kafkaesque'. A person who learns to situate himself becomes increasingly specific, particular, as the list of those on whom he depends and who depend on him grows longer. There lies the whole paradox of holobionts, or of the sociology of associations: getting more and more familiar with someone means travelling ever further towards those that person is involved with. The individual reduced to almost nothing is bound to feel powerless in the face of the immensity of all that dominates him; the person, the actor-network, the actant-people, the holobiont, feels himself grow wings as the items on his list, in his course of action, on his *curriculum vitae,* multiply; they disperse, they

87

proliferate. There are 'ties that free': the more the individual depends, the less free he is; the more the person depends, the more scope he has for action. When he seeks to spread his wings, the individual constantly comes up against his limits, moans and groans, overwhelmed by forlorn passions, there's scarcely anything left for him to do but feel indignation and resentment; when the person stretches out, repopulates himself, gets some distance, he *scatters*, in the strict sense of the word, he shares himself, mixes, and step by step recovers powers to act that he never imagined. Clearly, the 'monstrous insect' is not the one people thought! It's Gregor who takes flight, and his parents who waste away in their box.

This kind of compass doesn't just *orient* whoever stands in it, it *repairs* a principle of engendering that was broken. The erstwhile modern 'subject' didn't know *where* to stand in space, all contorted as he was, immobilised, and indeed half-blind, so that he could stay facing 'objects' equally discombobulated, left hanging, led astray by having to be exposed to the public gaze – like the head of St John the Baptist on Salome's plate, to take up the example cited by Louis Marin. But this modern subject also doesn't know where to stand *in time*. Obviously, since, to fit into the cube, he had to break with his past – and even with the act of passing. Not just make a radical break so as to become 'resolutely modern', but agree *to pass up the means of passing*. Deprived upstream as well as down, the 'modern subject' can't backtrack in order to find the well-spring of action he'll need when he realises he's gone astray. This is the source of his distress: in order not to be tempted to backtrack, in order not to risk being considered 'reactionary', he has *burned his bridges*. The future has turned the past into a nightmare and opened up an unbridgeable chasm between the two. Horribly, the modern subject can only forge ahead, no matter what the consequences. And so, obviously, he can only cling doggedly to error, something rightly said to be the work of the devil. So that's it, he can no longer have any experience of the world, he has well and truly *made life impossible* for himself. It's precisely this void that devices like 'standing in the compass' are trying to fill.

When they encounter terrestrials, old-school progressives always accuse them – this really makes me laugh – of wanting to 'go back to using candles'. And it's true in fact that, if the Moderns burned their bridges so as to rule out the possibility of retracing their steps, there are probably only a few candles left in the boxes wrecked by the fire! But we terrestrials are not reduced to a few bits of wreckage. Saying that we've gone back to being 'archaic' is an understatement, we've become totally unused to resorting to the axe of 'modernisation'. So there's nothing stopping us from *backtracking*, since we refuse to ignore the engendering concerns of all those we depend on, upstream, and who depend on us, downstream. For us, the two are finally once more linked. The despised word 'tradition' doesn't scare us; we see it as a synonym for the capacity to invent, to pass on and, so, to carry on. We're trying to re-tie the Gordian knot that the sword of modernisation cut, and we're doing this by remembering the ways lifeforms have of staying alive. You've [*vous*] never sought to leave the earth, either. You've never had any compass needle other than Gaia. You're still the sons of Adam, human beings, made of dust perhaps, like humus, overloaded, over-flowing, multifaceted, overlapping, and maybe finally *capable of reacting* to the unexpected consequences of your actions.

Mortal bodies are piling up

What I find curious is that, though many of us realise that the landscape can get moving again, that the economy can finally be superficial, that even Gaia behaves quite differently from the famous 'inert things' of which 'Nature' was the assumed assemblage, people still persist in getting me to believe I 'have' a 'biological' body.

Monday, I was at La Salpêtrière hospital in Paris for a fresh injection of Taxol®; Tuesday, an excellent acupuncturist, who actually refers to himself as 'a bit of a wizard', stuck hot needles in my calf, giving off a sweet scent of sagebrush; Wednesday morning, Laetitia Chevillard, my qi gong coach, got me to breathe slowly so I could learn to send my energy to my right foot; but that afternoon, my nephrologist, this time across the way at La Pitié, studied my personal records online and decided my kidney was finally doing pretty well; and then on Friday, I saw a new specialist, a cardiologist, who wanted to do a scan but had to send me away with two new medications to slow down my heart, because it was beating too fast for the examination to be possible.

This experience is perfectly ordinary but, with what I've learnt about the reversal of the landscape, I wonder if I shouldn't also start freeing my body. Thanks to being locked-down, you [*vous*] feel an urge to liberate yourself absolutely and to switch metaphysics altogether.

Once, of course, I'd have accepted having a 'biological' body conceived as the 'material' base, the indisputable foundation, to which I'd have accepted adding my body *lived* from the inside, the inside of my subjectivity. This is what used to be known as following the 'psychosomatic' effects – your heart beats too fast because of anxiety, the needles act through an inner sensation of redistributed energy, and so on. But this way of distributing values, I've realised, doesn't do justice to Earth: its materiality is constituted quite differently from old-fashioned 'matter'. Of course, we can create little reservoirs, segments, sequences of Universe, more or less all over the place, at great expense, by mobilising a lot of human resources. But those reservoirs are never numerous enough, autonomous enough, not in the critical zone anyway, to form a continuous fabric resembling the *res extensa* of the philosophical tradition. It's more of an archipelago, a leopard skin, a patchwork cloak. As for the flow of the terrestrial world, it's composed of interlocking living things, all tangled up within the sediments of their actions – mountains and oceans, air and soil, cities and ruins.

Confusing surface and background, foreground and middle distance is like taking the agribusiness for a revelation of what constitutes a particular soil. I get the impression that almost everyone, these days, knows the difference between the two: thanks to various inputs and to outsourcing all the detrimental consequences

– poisoned peasants, accelerated erosion, eutrophical rivers, eradicated insects – we can easily obtain higher yields for a time, but that particular field is clearly driven out, expelled, launched into *above-ground* orbit. Far from expressing the profound nature of what a landscape could become, this seizure appears more and more for what it is: *a land grab*, violent confiscation, occupation, for a time, by others and especially for others, before they flee elsewhere, leaving behind the ravaged surface of the land. You only have to follow the agronomists to smell the difference, sometimes at just a few metres' distance, between a field lifted up by the agribusiness and flung into the air, and soil left lying fallow and thickened up by the many living things that compose it. And when I say 'smell', yes, I do indeed mean using your nose, after some soil scientist has shown you [*vous*] how to roll a clod of soil in the palm of your hand.

So, it's a matter of redistributing the continuous and the discontinuous, of reversing the foreground and the middle distance. In spite of its name, the 'extended thing', the *res extensa*, defined as the world's background ever since Descartes's philosophical novel first appeared, has only managed to *extend itself* locally and over certain segments or portions of our courses of action. In the case of agriculture, it is shrinking like Balzac's shrinking hide, or like a diminishing asset, to the point where the expression 'modern agriculture' has started to designate a quirk of the past . . .

But then, why is it that Monday's oncologist, Wednesday afternoon's nephrologist, and Friday's cardiologist behave as if all they'd done was pick out three distinct organs from *one and the same body*, my 'biological' body? And, on top of that, why am I meant to refer Tuesday's acupuncturist and Wednesday morning's coach to my psychology and to the effects this is supposed to induce, somewhat mysteriously, via some 'pineal gland' (another nice invention of the same René Descartes)? Besides, if I've followed their way of proceeding correctly, the only continuity they've covered is the one consisting of the online data base they consulted in all seriousness. Hence my impression that the continuity of my organs forms something more like a *map* based fairly superficially on the *territory* of a body accessible by other procedures – needles or breathing exercises. In which case it's the same for a body as it is for a field: the differences captured by biologists don't express my body's agencies any more than the agribusiness expresses the behaviour of a soil. Here, too, the map is not the territory seen from below and the right way round.

I'm not complaining about the power of medicine: I'm not criticising the ridiculous reductionism; I'm just trying to make my body compatible with what I've learned of Earth. Even if it's not about reviving the age-old analogy between microcosm and macrocosm, I would still like to make these work in concert. If it's true that we never have the experience of encountering 'inert things', then this must be even more true of our encounter with our own bodies! I'm not claiming, either, that the doctors chop my body into pieces, like butchers would a piece of beef, while the acupuncturist and the coach grasp it *in toto*, in 'wholistic' fashion. My body is no more a coherent whole than Gaia is. My body is no more a unique 'organism' than Earth is a living 'organism'. To grasp it 'as a whole' makes no more sense than extracting a 'part' of it, and hoping that this part will remain functional. If an isolated 'pound of flesh' doesn't make sense, neither does a 'whole body'. Uniqueness, edges, boundaries are what living beings most lack – and this goes for parts, of course, but also for wholes. That is indeed what the word 'holobiont' tries to capture: heterotrophs, by definition, cannot stabilise what they depend on. Give them an identity, and this latter will necessarily be out of whack with all the beings who authorise, contest, support, build up this temporary membrane. This goes for the entity 'heart', or 'kidney', as well as for the entities 'astral body', 'energy zone', 'aura' or 'acupuncture points'. The whole advantage of the lockdown is to free us from edges with clear lines.

Gregor, come [*tu*] to my rescue: your parents have a 'biological' body plus a 'psychology', fine. But you who've undergone this metamorphosis I'm trying to grasp, a hundred years on – what body should you get used to living inside?

I note that already, in calling on Earth, the 'biological' has shifted a bit. It has once again become dependent on instruments, laboratories, examinations, data bases, research, clinical trials, and is *reduced* to local samples, partial data captures, access protocols, some of which function as predicted, others not so much. This is the only useful sense of the word 'reductionism': whatever laboratory procedures allow us to capture. As a result, there are so many gaps, discontinuities between these islands, these archipelagos, these Sporades, that we now have no trouble adding a good dozen other professions, other apparatuses, coaches and acupuncturists, wizards and scarificators, each with his own tools, rationales and ambitions, but not one of whom is capable of 'covering' the experience of being a body. There is now room for everyone.

But this still doesn't tell us how to describe this flow of experience against which all these different professions later stand out. Well, I need to do this to ensure compatibility between the experience of living confined in and with Gaia, and that of living confined in and with my body. There's no point in getting used to no longer leaving Earth, while continuing to claim that, ideally, it would be so good, and vaguely possible, to leave my 'biological' body in order to be, I don't know, 'really myself' somewhere else . . .

Before, I used to say 'lived body' to refer to the subjective capture of the same set of things seen from inside, while my real body, my 'objectified' or even 'reified' body, as they used to say in the old days, remained solidly 'biological'. I'd now like to be able to use the term 'lived body' to point to the multitude of living things that gather together temporarily in fairly durable fashion so as to allow me to prolong my existence for a while. The experience of cancer has an intriguing side which is that it forces us to take an interest in the independence of a few of these beings that go their own way even more freely than the rest. Minute, inaccessible, cunning, obstinate, but above all, like all other living beings, following a law they give themselves. *Sui generis*, cause in itself, is a term used of all agencies and of Gaia, par excellence. This cloud of holobionts, these billions of overlapping, interlaced, interdependent agencies each lead their own life and each, according to its choices, endures or disappears, engenders or is wiped out. The lived body, the body of living beings, and thereby the body of mortals, now designates the very materiality of what I am. This is true of my interior as of my exterior, of the old 'subjective' body as of the old 'objective' body. If the oxygen I breathe comes from bacteria, the lungs that breathe it come from these immensely long lineages that have latched on to them as if they were a stroke of luck. And as for me, it's my luck to surf for a while on this immense wave that I refer to as 'my body'.

Isn't that a good way of ensuring the continuity of experience or, as Stengers says, of 'reclaiming common sense'? That was the inspiration behind the great alternative philosophical tradition of last century, the tradition spearheaded by William James and Whitehead. Having a body means learning to be *affected*. The antonym for 'body' is not 'soul, or 'mind', or 'consciousness', or 'thought'; it is 'death' – just as the antonym for Gaia is Mars, the inert planet. But this admirable tradition remained precisely alternative or dissident, lost in the formidable exile of positivism, inaudible in the racket made by the 'Great Acceleration'. If it's becoming audible again today, that's because our experience has once again become the – vernacular – experience of engendering. The macrocosm is helping renew the microcosm. If engendering practices ensure continuity, it's not through the playing out of relationships of cause and effect, which is always local, but because those practices introduce into all hiatuses in courses of action, into every detail, the moment, the void, the inspiration, the sometimes tiny burst of creativity that allows the most ordinary machinations – those of cells, genes, employees, doctors, robots themselves – to prolong for a bit longer their powers to act as well as to suffer. For half a century, it just so happens that it's been through the various brands of feminism that the demands of the body have gradually spread – *Our bodies, Ourselves* – to the point of slipping into all the interstices of the *res extensa*. They have done this firstly in critical fashion before going on step by step to occupy centre stage, and finally, thanks to their formidable resonance with Gaia, to become the fabric of the world and the new default position. We are all, male and female, engendered and mortal bodies who owe our conditions of liveability to other engendered and mortal bodies of all sizes and of all lineages.

11

The return of
ethnogeneses

Through the difficult ordeal of lockdown, terrestrials are now working out where they are, they're getting their bearings more and more accurately, they've invented their own metrics for getting around: meticulous exploration, based on trial and error, of what they depend on, and careful attention paid to engendering practices. They even have mortal bodies at last. But only to stumble across a new enigma: how many of them are there? Do other societies like them exist? Can they revisit the issue of belonging to a nation that has recognisable borders? On that score, Kafka's novella tells us nothing, Gregor having died alone, wasted away under his divan, without leaving any testimony about his congeners.

The difficulty is all the greater as all these terms like 'soil', 'territory', 'people', 'tradition', 'land' and 'going back to the land', 'rootedness', 'positioning', 'organicity' were appropriated and colonised by the Moderns to describe the past, the archaic, the reactionary, whatever we needed to tear ourselves away from, at any cost, by a mighty push towards the future. Taking them up again means covering oneself in the poisoned shirt of Nesses, and the burning sensation is all the more stinging as these same terms have been adopted, this time *positively*, by those who've effectively agreed to backtrack, to recover the protection of a homeland, a nation, a soil, a social enclave for a people, an ethnicity, an idealised past. 'If globalisation no longer leads anywhere anymore,' they cry, 'then at least give us a safe place to live in, where we'll be locked-down maybe, but protected, and more importantly, *on our own*.' The anti-Moderns are following the injunction proposed by the Moderns – just the other way round.

How can terrestrials make 'light' of belonging to the earth when they're actually aspiring to settle here permanently at last? How do we make Earth a credible base if the land has already been appropriated and reterritorialised by those who are carving it up among themselves into so many juxtaposed nations with no common ideal other than the war of each against all? They're in danger of looking as silly as the hero of David Brin's *The Postman*, who ambles along on his own claiming to represent a state long vanished, with no weapons but his cap, his epaulettes and his postie's bag, full of letters that have no authors or addressees. Terrestrials can't explore the rest of the world by presenting themselves as the last representatives of a universal state that no longer exists … But what, in fact, would inventing a new universal mean?

Let no one come along and accuse us, us terrestrials, of calling the universality of humanity into question. That has already been done, and on a massive scale. Anti-humanism is a game being played everywhere at once. It was furthermore inevitable that the end of Modernisation be translated into one huge mess, since Modernisation offered a common horizon of sorts, after all, an ersatz Omega Point. Once that anchor is ripped away, everything goes to the dogs. This negative universal shows up every day, from one crisis to the next, in the systematic deconstruction of what used to be called the 'international order'. For the moment, we must admit, the ruins of Modernisation look pretty much like a scene imagined by David Brin. Hence the impression that we're emerging from a lockdown only to enter into a new nightmare.

And yet, the old solution no longer seems adequate to pacify nations at war, as it was in the days when they'd say: 'Come on, we're all humans on this earth, that's what unites us.' That solution was understood in two ways, which both equally led us offshore. 'We're all humans' meant: 'Through our conscience, our ideals, our morality, we all equally escape the fate of inert things, biological bodies and animals.' Which boiled down to living precisely everywhere except with Earth! We had to believe in the Heaven, secular or religious, to which we would all finally decamp, by modernising ourselves in concert. But the other rendering of this lofty adage didn't allow us to localise ourselves on earth any more than the first did: 'We are all natural beings, produced by the same causes, and destined for the same ends as objects made of matter; let's modernise ourselves completely by disappearing without further ado, the way Nature does.' That process of naturalisation involved the same accelerated flight beyond Earth, the same uprooting from the soil, yet a different translocation, not to Heaven this time, but to the Universe, as we swung wildly to the other side, way beyond the *limes*. A double exile, double flight, in return for recognition of a universal humanity. We all modernised ourselves, yes, but at the cost of collective suicide! It was a high price to pay. Our death wish was such that it's not surprising themes of collapse were so swiftly popularised – as if they met a hidden desire for total collapse.

Curiously, the lockdown is helping terrestrials flee beyond the flight out of this world. This is why the great issue of anthropology is quietly making itself heard everywhere – the issue of mutual recognition of emerging nations who are wondering what being human with Earth means. If the situation has become a little clearer, in spite of everything, this is because, without our realising it, the work of *ethnogeneses* has resumed, as the disconnect between the 'human' universal and the material conditions of earthly life has become more pronounced. It's as if we now had to begin reckoning with different planetary regimes; as if humanity really had resigned itself to living on different planets; as if no one deluded themselves anymore about their ability to unify the human race. I'm reduced to inventing a sort of astrology, spotting auspicious or inauspicious alignments of celestial bodies that have become more and more incommensurable.

There is the planet *Globalisation*, which continues to attract those who do indeed hope to be able to modernise in the old-fashioned way, even if the land they live on is actually disappearing. Being 'humans', for these people, means remaining gleefully indifferent to the fate of the planet, by denying the fragile, filmy existence of its critical zone. In the twentieth century, such globalisation delineated the common horizon, but these days it looks to be nothing more than a provincial version of the planetary. Hard to universalise this denial of reality – at least on earth.

There is the planet that could be called *Exit*, inhabited by those who've understood the earth's limits all too well, but who, for that very reason, have decided to get off it, at least virtually, by inventing hypermodern bunkers for themselves on Mars or in New Zealand. For these people, the word 'human', in its full sense, is reserved exclusively for the rich, the famous 0.01 per cent. The ideal of modernisation for all has been abandoned and that of the redoubtable Ayn Rand once and for all realised. At last, not to have to worry about anybody! Those they've agreed to leave in the lurch, the *left behind*, are known merely as 'supernumeries'.

Lastly, there is the planet *Security*, the one peopled by social rejects who group together in solidly confined nations that are also completely offshore, but which said rejects hope are at least protective. 'Humans', in this particular world, isn't a particularly widespread term, since it gets replaced by 'Polish', 'Northern Italians', 'Hindus', 'Russians', 'White North Americans', 'Han Chinese', 'native-born French', as the case may be. Everyone is careful not to apply the term to those living beyond the borders. The ideal of a common humanity has been thrown overboard.

If, in this terrible conjunction, terrestrials don't feel completely crushed, that's because of the powerful attraction of a fourth planet. It's perilous to give this one a name too soon if we want to avoid letting ourselves be captured by the gravitational field of mournful modern history. This particular planet is not 'archaic', nor of course 'primitive', not even 'fundamental' or 'ancestral'. It's the one inhabited by countless peoples who, as Viveiros de Castro says, have always lived *this side of* the Moderns – something that has allowed them largely to maintain their vernacular ways of life, resisting the developers as best they can. Now some of these extramoderns have stepped out of their boxes and deconfined themselves or, rather, decolonised themselves at full speed. So completely that we'd be tempted to name their planet *Contemporary*, since it's gone from being obsolete to being very much *of our time*. As Nastassja Martin puts it rather bluntly, it's from these peoples, who we put in danger, that the industrialised can now learn how to survive, as if, to civilise themselves anew, they'd said to themselves: 'Let's be resolutely *rewilded* by these guys' . . .

But then, attracted and repulsed by these four attractors as terrestrials are, what could their plans be? The machine for engendering peoples who gropingly set out to explore who they are, with whom, against whom and for whom, requires an art that Stengers calls *diplomacy*.

Of course, nation-states already practise diplomacy, but on territories that are lopsided, since there's never any overlap between what lies inside their borders and what lies outside but nonetheless allows them to prosper. If nation-states appear side by side, *partes extra partes*, on a map, this is because we don't know how to draw the shadow states that make them liveable and in which they find themselves, in a way, enfolded. There's such a thing as 'international relations' and there are even a few supranational machines, but these haven't managed to reduce the formidable disconnect, daily more pronounced, between the territories 'we live on' and those 'we live off'. And so, diplomats never know exactly what the interests of their constituents are – the most decent diplomat risks betraying them.

It's no good hoping to open up the nation-states by celebrating the 'local', since it's the same grid that determines the scale proper to the states and the scale proper to the territories embedded in those states, while even a cursory exploration of interdependencies forces us to go from one scale to the other, and to do so several times a minute. Nothing is strictly local, national, supranational or global. We'd need to define as many maps as there are agencies: every river, every town, every migratory bird, every earthworm, every anthill, every computer, every supercontainer, every cell, every diaspora defining a form that superimposes itself, slobbers, spills over the others while concealing all their ins and outs. What a shamozzle that would be!

Should we frankly abandon all pretension to humanism? That's very tempting now that lifeforms are running in the same direction. And yet, what an evasion it would be to abandon anthropocentrism at the very moment when modernised humans, in their number, in their injustices, in their well and truly universal expansion, are starting to weigh up the fate of other lifeforms – to the point of being seen, in certain calculations, as the agents of a sixth extinction. As Clive Hamilton indignantly points out, this is surely not the moment for those particular humans to throw off the burden that their multifarious presence has put on all other living beings. People may well be right to criticise 'Anthropocene' as a term, but it exactly tags the goal we need to attain once we see that embracing anti-humanism would be going from bad to worse, another way for Atlas to abandon the mission he recklessly took on. He can't get rid of this crushing burden just by shrugging his shoulders – *Atlas shrugged all over again*? If the myth of Atlas still means anything, it's more about lifting the weight that certain peoples have put on the others.

If the machine for engendering peoples is clogging up on all sides, that's because terrestrials never stop wrestling with the very notion of borders, whether local, national or universal. We can measure just how far modern humans are offshore, when we realise that their mental resources rely exclusively on identity and its boundaries. That's like treating heterotrophs – those who depend on other lifeforms to exist – as if they were autotrophs, autochthons and autonomes. And that's where the chaos springs from. It's easy to understand the function of diplomats mandated by the Westphalian States to negotiate border lines, but what would a *diplomacy for holobionts* look like? And yet it's in the very nature of diplomacy to be able to grasp *the limits of any notion of limits*. As far back as the history of this so very ancient art goes, the possibilities of negotiation have always relied on redefining the famous 'red lines' that parties never cease drawing in the sand, with the help of any number of threats. As if they knew for sure what they were attached to and what they wanted! As if they had an identity! As if they knew how many external beings the fine membranes, inside which they believe themselves to be protected, depended on. Every time, the subtle art of diplomats relies on modifying interests by modifying identities. Holobionts, those overlapping monads, can't be made to fit inside borders. We may as well try and part the sea with a sword, according to Leibniz, who is not for nothing the patron saint of diplomacy, as well as the father of monads.

So, we have to go about it differently. A path opens before us when we realise that the universal doesn't proceed in the same way with Earth as it does within the Universe. It's not a problem of scale, as if we had to go progressively from the local to the global, from the small to the big, from the specific to the general. It's a question of metrics. The universals whose evolution is now suspended borrowed their modes of behaving from ways of being in the Universe: one case could stand in for all cases. The 'royal sciences' have accustomed us to these striking generalisations: Descartes had no sooner stabilised a few results to do with measuring a light ray than he was writing *The World*; Pasteur had no sooner injected an anti-rabies vaccine into Joseph Meister than the hygienists were already declaring the 'end of infectious diseases'; Sony gets the heads of two anthropomorphic robots to nod, and *voilà*, posthumanism is already declared to have arrived! The Moderns could never check a fact or promote a technique except by combining the ideal of objective knowledge with magic. They were always looking for a *magic bullet*.

Well, with Earth, that is not how things contaminate each other, conspire, spread, interlock, complicate each other and, yes, in actual fact, spread – only, *step by step*, counting on the support of other overlapping beings and without ever skipping a phase. The sciences meander about Earth slowly, without the aid of magic. Old-school universals, taken from the Universe, have no currency on Earth. Oh, what a fine lesson Covid-19 has given the locked-down, by reminding them that an agent such as a virus could once proceed perfectly well from mouth to mouth and from hand to hand and whizz round the world several times in a few months.

Now, there's a globaliser for you! At least, thanks to the pandemic, no one will say anymore that 'step by step' inevitably means we will always be 'local' and 'clearly distinct' from each other.

As a result, we're not completely helpless. The arts of diplomacy have simply recovered their original vocation by continuing to grope their way through trial and error, knowing that every limit conceals another, and that every change of scale presupposes relaying by another living thing. Earth has clearly ended up insinuating itself just about everywhere, so why couldn't those who follow its modes of proliferation also manage to spread? Slowly, of course, and without being able to skip over conflicts. After all, Gaia wasn't born *big*, either: it became big, from one moment to the next, from one invention to the next, from one artifice to the next.

12

Some pretty strange battles

Getting the hang of lockdown means learning lessons from it for what comes next, as if Covid could serve as preparation, as a dress rehearsal, for when we will once again be locked-down by some other panic in the face of some other threat. The longer lockdown goes on, the more it proceeds by fits and starts, the harder the lesson, but also the more lasting: we won't go outside again! Outside is a different envelope, a different biofilm, a different critical zone, one that does indeed find itself in a critical state. 'End of the line; all change please.' Between yesterday and today, between Gregor, the good son and good employee, and Gregor, the bug trying to control the erratic movement of his six hairy legs, there is such an abyss that there's a chance his heart will fail him if he recalls bygone times, modern times.

And it's this feeling of confinement that you're [*tu*] trying so hard to give a *positive* spin? That amounts to making fun of us! At the very moment when we're suffocating behind our masks and we're being asked to stay two metres apart from all these hemiplegic faces, our families, our nearest and dearest? But we want to do the opposite, we want to breathe freely, at the top of our lungs, to forge ahead, go back to being carefree, yes – and even get on a plane!

There, no need to go far to recognise new lines of conflict: they cut across our lungs. We want to breathe like before, while those who claim to be 'carrying on like before' are smothering us – and we *conspire* with them. The whole planetary respiratory system is disrupted and at all levels, whether it's a matter of the masks we're gasping behind, the smoke from fires, police repression or the sweltering temperature imposed on us, all the way up to the Arctic. The cry is unanimous: 'We're suffocating!' And we can hear this particular cry, at least, just as well in Gregor's closed room as in the poky little kitchen where the Samsa family goes to ground.

I don't just sense this war of each against all through one country's occupying another, as in the past, but through the undue occupying of one or other of the beings that allow me to subsist. This particular insect, this chemical product, this metal, this atom – yes, it's down to atoms – to say nothing of the climate – ah, the good old climate which we'd like so very much to forget about but which will never let go of us . . . And that occupation, that land grab is multifaceted and on all levels. Inevitably, since every citizen lives in a world that is not the one that *provides for him*. Holobionts can never define themselves by their identity, since they depend on everything else to have an identity. By definition, they are always out of whack, overlapping with others they depend on.

Every time I'm contacted by an activist, a citizen of a nation-state, we become aware together that the boundaries of our identities, of our governments, of our products, of our technologies, and of course of our inner selves, are irrelevant. As the case may be, my nephew realises he needs grape-pickers by mid-August to harvest his grapes; my daughter, that her intestinal microbiota depend on food she used to turn her nose up at; my friend, that his windscreen doesn't have any of the insects that used to pollinate his fruit trees on it anymore; my next-door neighbour, that the rare earths she needs for her factory are all in China's hands; all the above, ultimately, that the temperature of the atmosphere depends on every one of their daily actions, and so on. Every encounter is an ordeal undergone by borders within which the action of an agent used to unfold till now. They're overrun every time by other agents that encroach on what used once to demarcate a territory. And this further increases the duration, intensity and anxiety of being confined, and gives us the impression of always having to repel occupying powers.

So I find myself between two worlds: the one I live in as a fully fledged citizen, protected by rights, and this other enclosure, much more vast, more or less easy to determine, but fuller and fuller and more remote: the world I live *off*. Like two enclosures that are at once close and yet disconnected. The political, moral and emotional question for me then becomes: what to do with this *second world*? What does it mean to extend the borders of my country, my people, my nation, so as to *include* this second world such as it is gradually revealed to me? Do I become an inhabitant of another political body? This is where ethnogenesis begins to seriously dissolve my former affiliations. I no longer know which country is mine. I no longer recognise my soil. I'm lost.

Some pretty strange battles

Every bit of my body, of my niche, of my territory is occupied by others, luckily or unluckily for me. I'm perfectly happy to have friends and enemies, but I'd like them to be organised into more or less recognisable lines, camps, fronts. I don't expect my adversaries to wear a uniform, but it would be good to be able to recognise them, all the same. There's nothing worse than this multipronged war in which militias seem to act without wearing any insignia, moving around in unmarked cars. The emitters of CO_2 – where are they? The bee destroyers – how do I know if they're not in my garden or even in my cupboards? The Covid-carriers – how do I detect them behind their masks, especially if they're 'asymptomatic'? The people profiting from oil-exploration subsidies – where do we unearth them?

I actually have a solution, which is to throw outside my borders things and beings I nonetheless really need to survive. It's the perfect solution: on the one hand, I continue to benefit from access to this second world; on the other, I refuse access for these other agents, human or otherwise, to any form of citizenship, recognition, or rights equal to my own. This refusal, of course, will put me in a precarious position, as Pierre Charbonnier says, since I'm going to have to keep *occupying* territories whose presence I otherwise *deny*. This is the actual position of the *extractor*: extreme violence in order to maintain occupation – whether we're talking about colonies or oil, rare earths or low wages – and an every bit as violent rejection of all responsibility, since the rights of the first world don't extend to the second. These are the two pincer movements of the *land grab*: the one appropriates, the other excludes. *Enclosures* are always formed again. But how am I going to be able to stand the tension? Extractivism drives you mad, for the only way of absorbing such a contradiction is to flee out of this world. I start with climate scepticism, but where will I end up? With the conspiracy theorists?

So then, is it these Extractors who are my enemies? No! Because I'm one of them, every minute of my life! If I were to separate from them, where would I go? Particularly as the other solution is even harder to take in your stride. Let's suppose that as a committed citizen I decide *to wrap* a new line, a new edge around both the world I live in and the world I live off at one and the same time, and then say of the unit thereby surrounded: 'This is my soil, this is my people!' What will happen? I still find myself in a precarious position, but this time in relation to the nation-state of which I was till now a more or less carefree citizen. I become a traitor in the eyes of those who reject the inclusion of countless migrants – human or otherwise – in the definition of my new citizenship. And conflicts will increase as I, as a good activist, extend my investigation, repopulate my new territory, mobilise more knowledge, multiply alternative experiments, and oppose more and more harshly the morals of the Extractors. I find myself, once again, thrown out of all affiliation.

What can we call people who are stateless, who have no homeland, because they want to insert the terrestrial homeland, or better still the mother-terrestrial-homeland, into the definition of their own countries? 'Anarchists'? Yes, because they reject the borders of the state where they were born. 'Socialists'? If you like, but how do we insert the lichens and forests and rivers, the humus and this eternal bloody CO_2 in the old notion of society? 'Citizens of the world', if the world could become the planet? 'Internationalists', if 'nation' could extend to non-humans? 'Interdependants'? 'Criticalzonists'? 'Loyalists'? 'Reconnectors'?

Even as the Extractors maintain occupation of the second world through violence and take flight in denial through another kind of violence, the *Menders* – I'm trying out this provisional name – have to battle to create another way of stitching together territories that their enemies have abandoned after having occupied and destroyed them. But they have to go about this mending job without any of the legal, police, state, mental, moral or subjective resources of the nation-state in which they still find themselves included – at least for the moment. And especially without the guaranteed support of countless entities from this second world they claim to embrace, but whose customs and creeds and demands they largely know nothing about. And to complicate matters still further, the overlap of holobionts means that behind every border another border shows up, another world of operators we knew nothing about beforehand and which we're going to have to take into account. Hence the many so-called 'environmental' controversies over each participant in a world that is no longer common at all: meat, atom, forest, wind turbine, vaccines, car, bricks, pesticides, fish, seed, river – everything is now a subject of conflict. But, here's the thing: these conflicts no longer organise themselves into a recognisable picture.

Over the previous two centuries, a huge machine was in place, an enormous scenography, that organised all conflicts and allowed people to work out, albeit roughly, where they needed to stand to try and be just. This was the conflict between rich and poor, a conflict made all the more precise by the distinction made between proletarians and capitalists. The new conflict between the Extractors and the Menders, if we accept the term, plays the same role today in its ubiquity, its intensity, its violence, its complexity, as the previous conflict, except that it mobilises many more living things than humans alone. To say it's global would be a euphemism. It has the world as its stake, except that the definition of the world differs radically according to the parties to the conflicts. Above all, it cuts across the old class lines in a whole host of cross-sections: we learnt this from the *Gilets jaunes*. The term *intersectionality* may well have come at the right time. Invented to capture the novelty of conflicts between humans, it's even better adapted to define the conflicts between Extractors and Menders whereby, for every different stake, the frontlines have to be redrawn and restitched, repaired, restored, patched up with other alliances on other territories.

The old scenography relied on the Economy since it was through their position in the 'production system' that injustices were spotted. But in these strange new battles, the Economy is no more than a superficial veil, and we're no longer dealing with production. What's at issue now are engendering practices and the possibility, or not, of maintaining, continuing, even ramping up the liveability conditions of lifeforms which, by their action, maintain the very envelope inside which history never ceases to unfold. Not just a history of the class struggle anymore, but a history of these new classes, alliances, sections struggling for the liveability that Nikolaj Schultz studies under the heading of 'geo-social classes'. The becoming-non-human of humans displaces injustice: it's no longer 'surplus value' that gets gobbled up, but our capacities for geneses, the surplus value of subsistence or engendering.

What about organising the war of the Extractors and the Menders into two camps? No! It can't be done, because the notion of a 'camp' only made sense in revolutionary periods, when people imagined *replacing* one world with another, radically, totally, through a great dialectical swing, through a sort of extreme operation, limited in time, consistent and concerted. But the appalling irony is that this replacement, this great swing *has already taken place*, and it's precisely this *replaced world*, the modernised world, that we want to get out of by getting back to our own – or what's left of it – so as to make it prosper. The Anthropocene is the name of this total revolution, and it happened under our very feet while we were celebrating, in that glorious year, 1989, the 'victory over communism'. There you have it, this strange defeat!

What makes all the current battles so very strange is that we really are at war, and it's a war to the death, a war of eradication; a war that I, nonetheless, feel incapable of organising into camps, into two camps, imagining the victory of one over the other. Especially as we'd need to believe in identities if we wanted to rally under the same banner, whereas it's precisely the limits of any notion of identity that the current crisis reveals. Enemies are everywhere and first of all in us, because they have actually insinuated themselves into our territories through the unexpected intermediary of things that have resumed their own movement – the movement we couldn't discern when they were taken for simple 'inert objects' and they actually remained at a distance. Whence the obligation to reconstitute the nature of the soil particle by particle, yes, to mend, when every detail of critical zones is a world in itself that involves us and forces obligations upon us.

And so, with my feet on the consortium's compass, I consult myself: in terms of my minuscule actions, do I enhance or do I stifle the lives of those I've benefited from till now? Their number never ceases to grow, as holobionts slot into each other at all levels and stretch out. There used to be a political culture, political affects, for 'forging ahead' and replacing this world with another, but, shatteringly, there is no such thing for *adjusting ourselves* to the Earth, for *ceasing to replace this world with another*. As if we needed to replace affects, attitudes, emotions, or even our sense of action. Oh, unhappy Moderns, how well we understand why you aspired to be old-fashioned humans again, free, liberated from all ties, on the road to progress, breathing at the top of your lungs, outside, yes, outside! Gregor's torment. And, yet, Gregor swiftly realised that giving in to that temptation would be the surest way to lose his soul – and we, ours.

13

Scattering in all directions

It's really weird, I know, to want to draw lessons from this repeat lockdown to the point of turning it into an almost metaphysical experience. And yet, it is indeed the physical – meta-, infra-, para- – that we're dealing with, because this ordeal has forced us to acknowledge that we don't yet know *where* we've been locked-down; that we don't feel the consistency, the resistance, the physiology, the resonance, the combining, the overlap, the properties or materiality of the things that surround us, the same way we used to do. While the Moderns hoped to change times, now they're obliged to re-learn how to situate themselves in space. Only two years ago, we organised seminars to try to probe the sources of insensitivity to the climate issue. Now, everyone knows that it is indeed an issue; but that doesn't mean we know how to react to it. This is because, behind the political question – 'What can we do? How can we get out of this?' – another question has cropped up: *'Where the hell are we?'* Thanks to the lockdown and even to these horrible masks that swallow up our faces and suffocate us, we've come to feel that behind the political crisis, a *cosmological* crisis has erupted. We never have encountered an 'inert thing', no more in the city, where everything is the work of living things, than in the country, where everything preserves traces of the action of living things.

This is not the first time this has happened, of course. The future industrial nations went through many mutations of the same order, especially at the turn of the sixteenth and seventeenth centuries. That's when those nations were dragged out of the old finite cosmos, where they felt like they were lying around confined, before being sent hurtling into the infinite Universe outlined by the violent seizure of the 'New World', a violence intensified by the stupefying discoveries made by scientists from Copernicus to Newton. Everything had to be overhauled – the law, politics, architecture, poetry, music, government and, of course, the sciences – to cope with this initial metamorphosis. And to accept the idea that the earth, having become a planet among others, had started turning. Ever since Galileo, the idea had indeed been that we were going to live in *another world*: the Universe, transferred, grafted, transplanted on to earth. But Earth is made of quite different matter. Yet another world revealed *beneath* the other world. Will history close in on itself once more? It's a history full of pitfalls. How can we curl up in this particular history without losing the plot?

The world is turning, once more, today, but this time *on* and *by* itself, and we find ourselves again in the middle of it, slotted in, confined in it, stuck in the critical zone, without being in any way able to make the same great gesture of liberation. I feel more like a load of washing in the drum of a washing machine, turning furiously, under pressure and at high temperature! We need to reinvent everything all over again – the law, politics, the arts, architecture, cities. But – and this is stranger still – we also need even to reinvent movement, the vector of our actions. We need to not forge ahead into the infinite, but to learn to *step back*, to *unplug*, in the face of the finite. That's another way of liberating yourself. A form of feeling your way, and, curiously, of becoming capable again of *reacting*. Yes, yes, I know, 'reacting' and 'reactionary' have the same root. Too bad! It was always forging ahead that shut us away, so now it's learning to step back that is de-confining us. We need to recover our capacities for movement, yes, our powers to act. It's always this becoming-an-insect that allows other forms of movement, as a crab, as a cockroach. There is beauty, there is dancing, in the rhythmic reptation of my Gregor.

Nothing shows this paradox more clearly than the excellent idea of calculating 'Earth Overshoot Day', a calculation that reveals a temporal rupture as marked as the spatial rupture. Even if it's perfunctory, this indicator allows us to endow each nation-state with an increasingly precise date that corresponds to the day of the year when the state's 'production system', to use an outmoded term, will have exhausted what the planet has provided for that state's use. To stay within the limits – or, at least, the current known limits – each state would have to *push back* the date as far as possible, ideally as far as 31 December. We're obviously not there. It seems that humanity, taken as a whole, overshot its limits on 29 July, then has gone on living the rest of the year till 31 December 'beyond its means', in debt to the planet – a debt of five months, deferred, obviously, carried forward to next year's assessment!

That gives an idea of the ubiquity and violence of the conflict between the Extractors and the Menders. In their indifference, the Extractors never cease bringing the overshoot date further forward in the year – if we let them have their way, we will have exhausted the whole year's resources before Candlemas. The Menders are trying to push it back as far as possible – ideally to New Year's Eve – which is what happened in the northern spring of 2020. Thanks to lockdown, we were able to record a *retreat* of three weeks in overshoot day. A very temporary retreat, which the year 2021 risks shifting again, only in the wrong direction, thanks to the 'economic recovery'. (It appears that other terrestrials, viruses of course, but also foxes, perch, otters, dolphins, humped-back whales, coyotes, took advantage of the retreat to cavort a little – and blackbirds, to get their singing better heard!)

We can gauge the violence of the power struggle between the Extractors and the Menders if we imagine the terrible ordeals that had to be undergone just to shift by a few weeks the overlap of the two worlds, the times we live in, and after that – the rest of the year – the times we live off and which we ignore. It takes a global economic crisis to claw back a few days – before losing them again! Nothing in the old scenography, when the parties to class conflicts unanimously backed 'production development', gives any idea of the scope of the tasks that need to be carried out by those who aim to 'push back overshoot day'. Especially when those who wish, on the contrary, to bring it forward are countless and powerful. Those tasks aren't about development anymore. Following the logic of lockdown, they're all about *envelopment*. How can we hang on to the idea of liberation if we have to accept slotting into, engaging in such contests? It's easy to understand the temptation to go back to being old-fashioned humans and to stick to the previous metamorphosis, the one offered by the 'Great Discoveries' celebrating escape to the infinite cosmos.

And yet – this is what's so amazing – we're all already there. We've all already mutated without realising, since the political horizon, what's known as the 'international order', is completely defined, explicitly and quite openly, by the challenge of maintaining the envelope in which present history unfolds, in a sphere, in a bubble, between limits, the limits defined for the moment by the famous two-degree rise in global temperature. The New Climate Regime is in fact a new political *régime*. You wouldn't think so, looking at national politics, and yet global politics has already tipped over to this other world that the confined have had a foretaste of and the deconfined are discovering with alarm. It's a world they will never leave, curved, circumscribed, held together by a sort of membrane, tent, sky, yes, atmosphere, conditioned air, which they'll have to live inside, among agencies that will never again take the form of a landscape of 'inert things'.

Amazing lag: while international politics has already shifted radically, the *scientific* source of this understanding of soil remains obscure. More than obscure: almost unutterable. And yet, why make those famous 'two degrees' the goal to be obtained by every global, national, local or personal decision, if the proof were not already surreptitiously accepted that Earth is indeed the hazardous product of a machinery of living things that has till now provided conditions of liveability and that we sense, through thousands of vague experiences, is today undermined by our actions? For us to be so scared of damaging it, we must have accepted as obvious fact the existence of a sort of fabulous 'thermostat' whose dial 'humanity' – that unlikely actor! – has access to in order to regulate it. A double feedback loop, the first involving living beings able to create their own conditions of existence, into which the second feedback loop is slotted: the action of these living beings among others that are so close and so different, friends and enemies, industrialised humans, on those same conditions of liveability. Double lockdown, double envelopment, double muddle.

Earth, or Gaia, is already organising the political horizon while its scientific existence is unknown, scorned or denied and its metaphysical consequences remain invisible. Drawing a parallel between the earth that turns in Galileo's sense and the earth that turns on itself in the sense meant by James Lovelock and Lynn Margulis, as I try to do in a hundred different ways with Frédérique Aït-Touati, means creating a bit of a scandal every time. For once, official policy – the famous climate accords – is ahead of scientific mindsets. People go on behaving as if it were a mere stroke of luck that organisms 'adapt' to their environment, as if they hadn't *provided* the latter for themselves, by making it favourable when it wasn't. And, consequently, as if they couldn't, in their turn, make it favourable or unfavourable depending on the action of these living beings among others that are human beings – living beings much too much in a hurry. It's not surprising that common sense is in tatters.

They're asking us to act as if we were living with Earth, when they're doing everything they can to see that we move out of it. Bit of a contradictory order! Regime crisis, indeed, if what we mean by that is that it's all about a *planetary* regime.

Earth exercises an authority that thwarts, disrupts, contests the modes of sovereignty of the nation-states that organised the carving up of land in the modern era. Oh no, it's not a matter of a sovereignty from above that's swooped down and globalised those of the states into a single incontestable power, a sort of ersatz 'global government'. It's that Earth is not global. Its mode of behaving, of expansion, of contamination has scarcely changed since the first bacteria succeeded in covering our ancestral planet with a film a few centimetres thick. This film has got thicker, bigger, more spread out, but always step by step, so that after four and a half billion years, it has still not exceeded the few kilometres of the critical zone. This particular contamination, this viral form of behaviour, simply can't be accommodated in the dazzling emblems of power imagined by the empires. No palace, pyramid, codex, prison, colonnade, dome or globe. No religion. No deification.

And yet, there is certainly the exercise, multifaceted and multiscaled, of that form of power that devolves on those who can describe themselves, collectively, as autonomes and autochthones. Autotrophs can only describe themselves, strictly speaking, as being from Gaia, the planet we can't overshoot and can never leave. In that sense, then, it's *sovereign*. But this sovereignty comes from below and through step-by-step concatenation. In spite of the presence of forms of the globe that always slip into its representation and are all borrowed from human empires, Earth is in no way englobing. We are confined to it but it's not a prison, it's just that we're *rolled up* in it. Freeing ourselves doesn't mean getting out of it. It means exploring its implications, folds, overlaps, entanglements.

There's no doubt that this extension of Gaia obliges us to divide up the forms of sovereignty that the states once monopolised. As if Gaia peeled them off, one after the other, so as to better redistribute them. Nothing surprising about that, since the delineation of political beings depends on the old cosmology, the one that held sway in the sixteenth and seventeenth centuries, in the days of Bodin and Hobbs. That's precisely the scale – in kilometres – that the nation-state tried to establish once and for all by squaring out the planet – in the old sense of a planetary body seen from above – through a cobbling together of countries in conflict or committed to fragile alliances. It's this localisation from above that lockdown has allowed every one of us to contest.

Well, terrestrials employ a different scale, that of connected lifeforms, which obliges them to constantly thwart, and, so, call into question, for each subject, the relationship between the small and the big, the demarcated and the interlinked, the swift and the slow. Since nothing involving Earth keeps inside state borders, and the international covers only a minuscule part of the stakes, the change in regime forces us to figure out what boils down to protection, to justice, to the police, or to trade, without necessarily condensing this within a national enclosure. All conflicts between Extractors and Menders are over such a redistribution of powers. Territories in desperate need of recognition are always *on both sides* of every border. Overshooting the limit of the notion of a limit is the new way of breaking free.

Curiously, in its way of proceeding from case to case, the law most closely resembles these forms of progressive and fragile universalisation. What, Earth's Law, the law of Gaia, the proper noun? Yes, a law that has always existed, which historians and anthropologists find traces of everywhere, but which has been ignored because it doesn't resemble either 'natural law' – 'nature' never having offered terrestrials a model – or the law of empires. A weak law, then, but one that is genuinely sovereign, the law that imposes limits on the notions of limits, the *nomos* of all the others. Motherland of law? *Sanctissima Tellus*, still impossible to recognise, to establish, but already present everywhere, from the moment terrestrials are no longer 'outside' but inside what overshoots them and continues to provide for them.

But, then, in wanting to celebrate this lockdown, in striving to place us under the sovereignty of Gaia, admit that you [*vous*] want to put an end to our history, yes, be honest and come out with it, to take our breath away, and even, to put it more brutally, castrate us. Where is innovation? Where is creativity? How are we going to recover luxury, comfort, prosperity? How are we going to go on celebrating that cherished word, freedom?

The Menders are tempted to reply: 'But who told you [*vous*] that terrestrials aren't also looking to prosper? Who says that we, too, don't want to be free, free at last to leave the place you've tried to lock us down in? If there's something we industrialised humans share with Gaia, it's not nature but artifice, the capacity to invent, the capacity not to obey laws other than the ones we've made for ourselves. Strangely, it's through technology that we best capture this inventive, scattered, modest, yes, modest, power that is Gaia's. Earth is not green, it's not primitive, it's not intact, it's not "natural". It's artificial through and through. We can feel ourselves vibrating with it in the city every bit as much as in the country, in a laboratory every bit as much as in the jungle. Nothing in the original conditions made its extension necessary, inevitable. Nothing in the current conditions make its continuation necessary, inevitable. It's in every innovation, in the details of every structure, of every machine, of every device, that Earth's intensity is most clearly revealed. For eons lifeforms turned only just a few of the original conditions to their advantage. The ingenuity of human beings keeps this whole process going, by mobilising more and more combinations of atoms, by going further and further down Mendeleev's Periodic Table. That doesn't make this ingenuity an enemy, quite the opposite. Innovation and artifice are what makes the world go around. Injustice and crime stem from the carefree attitude that makes people feel they can ignore the limits but not learn how to *turn them round*, because that's something that bacteria, lichens, plants, trees, forests, ants, baboons, wolves and even Vinciane Despret's octopus friends have been able to do just as well.'

So where does it lie, then, this sickness that has paralysed our capacities for invention by orienting them in a single direction offshore? Obviously it lies in this strange perversion that strives to orient invention towards a single goal by overshooting the limits so we can be hurtled out of this world instead of turning those limits round; or, even more perverse, that strives to set up heaven on earth. Two forms. The first is the pseudo-religious one of exiting this world, the other the pseudo-secular one of introducing heaven on earth. That was Ivan Illich's terrible warning: 'the corruption of the best is the worst'. That's not how Gaia was extended, prolonged, complicated, established. It's because Gaia wasn't seeking any goal that it ended up partly regulating itself. It opens out, breaks up, disperses. By forcing us to forge ahead, by dreaming we'll become post-humans, by imagining we're about to live 'like gods', can't you [*vous*] see that you're depriving us of the sole power of reorientation there is: groping, testing, going back over our failures, exploring? In the old world, it might have made sense to forge ahead, to make our way towards some Omega Point. But if we've tipped over into the new world, gone back inside living conditions whose remains we're obliged to mend, then the most important movement is to be able to scatter in all directions. If only we had the time.

So, you've [*vous*] landed, you've crashed, you've extricated yourself from ground zero, you're advancing, masked, your voice barely audible: like Gregor's, like mine, it's a sort of mumbling. 'Where am I?' What to do? Go straight ahead, as Descartes advised those lost in a forest? No! You should scatter as much as you can, fan out, explore all your capacities for survival, conspire, as hard as you can, with the agencies that have made the places you've landed on habitable. Under the canopy of the heavens, now heavy again, other humans mingled with other materials form other peoples with other living things. They are freeing themselves at last. They're coming out of lockdown. They're being metamorphosed.

14
A little further reading

Although written in the style of a philosophical fable –
the best way, in my view, of turning round the painful
ordeal of lockdown to digest the change in cosmology imposed by the New Climate Regime – this book
is based on a multifaceted collaboration with many
friends. In this final part I sum up, section by section,
the main research projects that have inspired me. I also
spell out the numerous overlaps that make any book an
assemblage of holobionts . . .

Many authors agreed to read me, notably Alexandra
Arènes, Anne-Sophie Breitwiller, Pierre Charbonnier,
Vivian Despoues, Jean-Michel Frodon, Emilie Hache,
Dusan Kasik, Frédéric Louzeau, Baptiste Morizot,
Nikolaj Schultz and Isabelle Stengers. Frédérique Aït-
Touati, Veronica Calvo, Maylis Dupont, Eduardo
Viveiros de Castro and Nikolaj Schultz. All went over
the manuscript in detail, some of them several times,
even. And, as always, for over twenty-five years, Philippe
Pignarre believed a book could defy the laws of gravity.
Many thanks to all.

A little further reading

1.

In Chapter 1, 'One way of becoming a termite', I use the French translation of Franz Kafka, *La Métamorphose*, Garnier-Flammarion, Paris, 1988, translated by Bernard Lortholary (the English version cited is Kafka, 'Metamorphosis', in *Metamorphosis and Other Stories*, Penguin Books, 1992, translated and edited by Malcolm Pasley). The notion of a 'line of flight' is taken, of course, from the book by Gilles Deleuze and Félix Guattari, *Kafka. Toward a Minor Literature*, University of Minnesota Press, Minneapolis and London, 1986, translated by Dana Polan (originally published 1975). For the overlapping voices of the characters from *Metamorphosis*, it's a good idea to listen to the opera by Michaël Lévinas, *Opéra de Lille*, 2011; an extract is accessible online at ictus.be/listen/michael-levinas-la-métamorphose (I'm indebted to Chantal Latour for this experience).

On termites, I was happy just to use my old copy of Edward O. Wilson, *The Insect Societies*, Belknap Press of Harvard University Press, Cambridge, Mass., 1971; but for ants, I draw on Deborah M. Gordon, *Ant Encounters: Interaction Networks and Colony Behaviour*, Princeton University Press, Princeton, 2010. As for the allusion, at the end of the chapter, to the difficulties in getting one's bearings, this refers to my book, *Où atterrir? Comment s'orienter en politique*, La Découverte, Paris, 2017, English version: *Down to Earth. Politics in the New Climatic Regime*, Polity, Cambridge, 2018, translated by Catherine Porter. That book still looked at the situation 'from above', before the ordeal of lockdown; in a way, this book is the post-crash report . . .

A little further reading

2.

In Chapter 2, 'Locked-down in a space that's still pretty vast', I try a thought experiment inspired by a visit from Jérôme Gaillardet, a geochemist from the Institut de physique du globe, Paris, in the course of an improvised sojourn of *vacances apprenantes*, or educational summer camps, at Saint-Aignan-en-Vercors. Jérôme has been my mentor for six years in the exploration of 'critical zones'. We're both trying to link the long history of the earth with the sciences that were once known in French as 'humaines' ('social' in English).

I am inspired here by my colleague Tim Lenton; in particular his book with Andrew Watson, *Revolutions That Made the Earth*, Oxford University Press, Oxford, 2011. To facilitate the experiment, I resort to Peter Sloterdijk's efforts to highlight the fact that it's impossible to 'get out of' the airconditioned enclosures proper to life itself. He provided a metaphysical expression of this finding in his trilogy, *Spheres*, and in particular in Vol. 2, *Globes*, Semiotext, 2014, translated by Weiland Hoban.

Interconnecting the 'artificial' city, the mountain landscape and the atmosphere, within the same 'interior' we can't get out of, is only possible provided we agree to take seriously the Gaia hypothesis on which I've been working for over fifteen years. Here, I sum up Timothy Lenton and Sébastien Dutreuil, 'What exactly is the role of Gaia?', in Bruno Latour and Peter Weibel (eds), *Critical Zone: The Science and Politics of Landing on Earth*, MIT Press, Cambridge, Mass., 2020, pp. 168–76. This sumptuous book, with layout by Donato Ricci, was compiled as a supplement to an exhibition of the

A little further reading

same name at the ZKM in Karlsruhe (July 2020–August 2021) and serves as a source for the present work. To grasp the impact of this shift in cosmology we need both to take inspiration from these new sciences and, at the same time, to absorb the shock of the new history and sociology of the sciences that I've been pursuing for forty years. In fact, these sciences are well and truly situated right inside the world they describe and transform. Hence the importance of 'illustrated knowledge' that refers us to this vital theme of the history of the sciences, summed up in my article, 'Les "vues" de l'esprit. Une introduction à l'anthropologie des sciences et des techniques', *Culture technique*, 14, 1985: 4–30 (accessible, like all my articles, on my website: bruno-latour.fr).

This theme is developed in Catelijne Coopmans et al., *Representation in Scientific Practice Revisited*, MIT Press, Cambridge, Mass., 2014, and magnificently developed in Lorraine Daston and Peter Galison, *Objectivity*, Princeton University Press, Princeton, 2010, as well as in Frédérique Aït-Touati, *Contes de la Lune. Essai sur la fiction et la science moderne*, Gallimard, collection "NRG essais", Paris, 2011. As for the concept of 'terrestrials', I introduced it in my *Facing Gaia: Eight Lectures on the New Climatic Regime*, Polity, Cambridge, 2017, translated by Catherine Porter (originally published 2015); it has the advantage of not specifying either the genus or species, just the local situation and the interlocking of the things beings are made up of.

It goes without saying that I madly oversimplify the distinction between Earth and the Universe, for the needs of my fable.

A little further reading

3.

Chapter 3, 'Earth is a proper noun', makes use of a contrast between two principles of positioning that play an essential role throughout the book. On the dangers of such a 'simple positioning', in the philosophical sense, see Didier Debaise, *Nature as Event: The Lure of the Possible*, Duke University Press, Durham and London, 2017, translated by Michael Halewood. But I also give it a more cartographical sense – see Valérie November, Eduardo Camacho and Bruno Latour, 'The territory is the map: Space in the age of digital navigation', *Environment and Planning D: Society and Space*, 28, 2010: 581–99 – drawing on the magnificent experiment conducted by Frédérique Aït-Touati, Alexandra Arènes and Axelle Grégoire, *Terra Forma. Manuel de cartographies potentielles*, B42, Paris, 2019.

To get used to the idea that we never experience 'inert things', not on earth anyway, it's useful to read Lynn Margulis and Dorian Sagan, *MICROCOSMOS Four Billion Years of Evolution from our Microbial Ancestors*, University of California Press, Berkeley, Los Angeles and New York, 1997 (originally published 1986). The curious return of the notions of the supralunar and the sublunar, traditional terms used in so-called 'pre-Copernican' cosmology, can be understood by comparing Alexandre Koyré's classic, *From the Closed World to the Infinite Universe*, Johns Hopkins Press, Baltimore, 1957, with, say, Timothy Lenton, *Earth System Science*, Oxford University Press, Oxford, 2016. Here, I've shifted the edge of the field, so to speak, by excluding the moon, which is a rerouting of the term.

A little further reading

In all his work, Baptiste Morizot strives to formulate Darwinism and to give animals back their agency; see in particular *Raviver les braises du vivant*, Actes Sud, Arles, 2020; and the review of it in 'Ce que le vivant fait au politique. La spécificité des vivants en contexte de métamorphoses environnementales', in Frédérique Aït-Touati and Emanuele Coccia (eds), *Le Cri de Gaïa. Penser avec Bruno Latour*, La Découverte, coll. 'Les Empêcheurs de penser en rond', Paris, 2021, pp. 77–118. The difference between 'life' and 'Life' is the subject of Sébastien Dutreuil's essay, 'Quelle est la nature de la terre', ibid., pp. 17–66.

To familiarise yourself with the notion of Gaia, you need to read James Lovelock's original books, especially the first one, *Gaia: A New Look at Life on Earth*, Oxford University Press, 2000 (3rd edn) (originally published 1979). But I benefited enormously from Sébastien Dutreuil's thesis, 'Gaïa, Hypothèse, programme de recherche pour le système terre, ou philosophie de la nature?', a doctoral thesis, Université de Paris I, 2016; and I drew on two recent articles to spell out the concept: Bruno Latour and Timothy Lenton, 'Extending the domain of freedom, or why Gaia is so hard to understand', *Critical Inquiry*, Spring 2019: 1–22; and especially Timothy Lenton, Sébastien Dutreuil and Bruno Latour, 'Life on Earth is hard to spot', *The Anthropocene Review*, 7, 3, 2020: 248–72.

On the mythological richness of Gaia as a concept, see Bruno Latour, *Facing Gaia*, op. cit., and especially Deborah Bucchi, 'Gaia face à Gaïa', in Frédérique Aït-Touati and Emanuele Coccia (eds), *Le Cri de Gaïa*, op. cit., pp. 165–84.

4.

I begin Chapter 4, '"Earth" is feminine – "Universe" is masculine', with the notion of a 'critical zone', drawing on Jérôme Gaillardet, 'The critical zone, a buffer zone, the human habitat', in Bruno Latour and Peter Weibel (eds), *Critical Zones*, op. cit., pp. 122–30. See also the whole of the third part of that book for a more complete rundown of the notion.

Our understanding of this zone owes much to the inventions of Alexandra Arènes, summed up in her article with Jérôme Gaillardet and me: 'Giving depth to the surface: an exercise in the Gaia-graphy of critical zones', *The Anthropocene Review*, 5, 2, 2018: 120–35, and in her thesis-in-progress at Manchester University.

The heterogeneity of critical zones is shown clearly by Susan Brantley et al., 'Crossing disciplines and scales to understand the critical zone', *Elements*, 3, 2007: 307–14, and by her contribution in Bruno Latour and Peter Weibel (eds), *Critical Zones*, op. cit., pp. 140–1. The limits of critical zones depend greatly on the temporality chosen.

This allows me to localise and dramatise a little the famous 'bifurcation of nature' commented on by Isabelle Stengers, *Thinking with Whitehead. A Free and Wild Creation of Concepts*, Harvard University Press, Cambridge, Mass., 2014 (originally published 2002). On the notions of a hiatus and the overlapping of agencies, see my *An Inquiry into Modes of Existence. An Anthropology of the Moderns*, Harvard University Press, Cambridge, Mass., 2013, translated by Catherine Porter.

On Gaia's limits, see 'Life on earth is hard to spot' and Tim Lenton and Andrew Watson, *Revolutions that Made the Earth*, op. cit. The localisation enabled by physics has been the subject of numerous essays in the history of the sciences, starting with Sharon Trawee, *Beam Times and Life Times: The World of High Energy Physicists*, Harvard University Press, Cambridge, Mass., 1988. Just a couple of examples: Peter Galison, *How Experiments End*, University of Chicago Press, Chicago, 1987, and the investigation of gravitational waves by Harry Collins, *Gravity's Shadow: The Search for Gravitational Waves*, University of Chicago Press, Chicago, 2004.

The links between neglecting engendering and obscuring the issue of gender are studied by Emilie Hache (director), *De l'univers clos au monde infini*, Editions Dehors, Paris, 2014; ditto, *Reclaim: Recueil de textes écoféministes*, Editions Cambourakis, Paris, 2016. On her most recent research, see 'Né-e-s de la terre. Un nouveau mythe pour les terrestres', *Terrestres*, 30 September 2020, terrestres.org. Adele Clarke and Donna Haraway, *Making Kin not Population: Reconceiving Generations*, Paradigm Press, Chicago, 2018, and Donna Haraway's book, *Staying with the Trouble: Making Kin in the Chthulucene*, Duke University Press, Durham and London, 2016.

5.

Chapter 5, 'A whole cascade of engendering troubles', follows the same problem of the composition of bodies within apparently very different realms. For more details, see Bruno Latour, Simon Schaffer and Pasquale Gagliardi (eds), *A Book of the Body Politic: Connecting Biology, Politics and Social Theory*, Foundation Cini, Venice, 2020; bit.ly/2zoGKYz.

A little further reading

I initially base what I say on Deborah Danowski and Eduardo Viveiros de Castro, 'L'arrêt de monde', in Emilie Hache (ed.), *De l'univers clos au monde infini*, op. cit., pp. 221–339, then on my article, 'Troubles dans l'engendrement', *Le Crieur*, 14, October 2019: 60–74, before extracting the notion of being out of whack in political economics from Pierre Charbonnier's important book, *Abondance et liberté. Une histoire environnementale des idées politiques*, La Découverte, Paris, 2020.

After that you can pursue the difference between autotrophs and heterotrophs and the long history of the earth in Lynn Margulis and Dorian Sagan, *MICROCOSMOS*, op. cit., and in Emanuele Coccia, *La Vie des plantes. Une métaphysique du mélange*, Payot, Paris, 2016.

The curious history of individualism is summed up here by my reading of Ayn Rand, *Atlas Shrugged*, Signet, New York, 1957. The Cartesian novel is the subject of a magnificent chapter, 'Cartesian romance', in Ayesha Ramachandran, *The Worldmakers: Global Imagining in Early Modern Europe*, University of Chicago Press, Chicago, 2015.

I pursue these links between biology and sociology in an article with Shirley Strum, 'Human social origins: Please tell us another story!', *Journal of Biological and Social Structures*, 9, 1986: 169–87. See also Bruno Latour, Simon Schaffer and Pasquale Gagliardi (eds), *A Book of the Body Politic*, op. cit. To follow the cascade in biology, you would do well to read Eric Bapteste, *Tous entrelacés*, Berlin, Paris, 2018; but you can learn the most about holobionts and the epigenetics they imply by reading the manual put out by Scott F. Gilbert and David Epel, *Ecological Development Biology: The Environmental Regulation of Development, Health and Evolution*, Sinauer Associates Inc., Sunderland, Mass., 2015. A simplified version of the thesis can be found in Scott Gilbert, Jan Sapp and Alfred Tauber, 'A symbiotic view of life: We have never been individuals', *Quarterly Review of Biology*, 87, 4, 2012: 325–41. On the folds of living beings between phages and viruses, I've learnt a lot from research conducted by Charlotte Brives, 'Pluribiose. Vivre avec les virus, mais comment?', *Terrestres*, 14 June 2020; terrestres.org/2020/06/01/pluribiose-vivre-avec-les-virus-mais-comment.

6.

Chapter 6, '"Here below"' – except there is no up above', conjures up the history of art. See for example Hans Belting, *La Vraie Image. Croire aux images?*, Gallimard, Paris, 2007, translated by Jean Torrent; and especially Louis Marin, *Opacité de la peinture. Essais sur la représentation au Quattrocento*, Usher, Paris, 1989. I pursue this issue of the religious image in my article, 'Quand les anges deviennent de bien mauvais messagers', *Terrain*, 14, 1990: 76–91, which was developed in the catalogue of the exhibition: Bruno Latour and Peter Weibel (eds), *Iconoclash: Beyond the Image Wars in Science, Religion and Art*, MIT Press, Cambridge, Mass., 2002; see in particular the article by Joseph Koerner, 'The icon as iconoclash', pp. 164–214. The notion that the religious has nothing to do with the 'spiritual' is taken up again in my book, *Rejoicing. Or the Torments of Religious Speech*, Polity, Cambridge, 2013, translated by Julie Rose.

A little further reading

On the strange history of the fusion of the heavens – the sky – and Heaven, I go with what Eric Voegelin calls 'immanentising' in *The New Science of Politics. An Introduction*, University of Chicago Press, Chicago, 1987 (first published 1951) – an idea also developed in my *Facing Gaia*, op. cit., Conference 6, pp. 239–83). I draw on Clara Soudan's thesis, 'Spells of our Inhabiting', Edinburgh, 1979. On a very similar notion, see Ivan Illich's amazing book, with David Cayley, *The Corruption of Christianity. Ivan Illich on Gospel, Church and Society*, CBC Ideas Transcripts, 2000. On ways of getting your bearings differently in the same places, I take up Anna Lowenhaupt Tsing, *The Mushroom at the End of the World: On the Possibility of Life in Capitalist Ruins*, Princeton University Press, Princeton, 2017; as well as her *Friction: An Ethnography of Global Connection*, Princeton University Press, Princeton, 2004.

It was clearly under the influence of Pope Francis's encyclical, *Laudato Si!*, 2015, that the issue of incarnation without the loophole of an 'other world' got going again. Taking up a suggestion of Eduardo Viveiro de Castro's, I devoured Vitor Westhelle's enigmatic book, *Eschatology and Space: The Lost Dimension in Theology Past and Present*, Palgrave, London, 2012. I pursue this research with Frédéric Louzeau and Anne-Sophie Breitwiller in relation to the Bernadines.

7.

Chapter 7, 'Letting the economy bob to the surface', draws on a great number of works. The notion of 'the Economy', with a capital 'E', comes from Timothy

A little further reading

Mitchell's major work, *Carbon Democracy. Political Power in the Age of Oil*, Verso. London, 2011. I owe my approach, in particular the notion of economisation, to my colleagues at the Centre de sociologie de l'innovation; see Michel Callon (ed.), *Sociologie des agencements marchands. Textes choisis*, Presses de l'Ecole nationale des mines, Paris, 2013, and his book *L'Emprise des marchés. Comprendre leur fonctionnement pour pouvoir les changer*, La Découverte. Paris, 2017; as well as Michel Callon, Yuval Millo and Fabian Muniesa (eds), *Market Devices*, Blackwell Publishers, Oxford, 2007. On the limits of production, see Marshall Sahlins's classic study, *Stone Age Economics*, Routledge, 1972, as well as that of David Graeber, *Debt: The First 5,000 Years*, Melville House, 2011, and Bruno Latour and Vincent Lepinay, *The Science of Passionate Interests: An Introduction to Gabriel Tardé's Economic Anthropology*, University of Chicago Press, Chicago, 2009.

Dusan Kazik's 'solution' comes from 'Plantes animées. De la production aux relations avec les plantes', his doctoral thesis at the Université Paris-Saclay prepared at AgroParisTech, 2020, and from his article, 'Le covid-19, mon allié ambivalent', AOC media, 16 September 2020. The idea that we need to break the spell of the Economy comes from Philippe Pignarre and Isabelle Stengers, *Capitalist Sorcery: Breaking the Spell*, Palgrave MacMillan, 2011 (originally published 2005). The freeing up of the notion of 'Nature' is analysed in detail in Karl Polanyi, *The Great Transformation: The Political and Economic Origins of Our Time*, Beacon Press, Boston, 2018, foreword by Joseph E. Stiglitz, introduction by Fred Block (first published 1944). The same perspective can be found in Baptiste Morizot, *Manières d'être vivant*, Actes Sud, Arles, 2020. The religious notion of the economy of nature is the subject of numerous works: see Giorgio Agamben, *The Kingdom and the Glory: For a Theological Genealogy of Economy and Government*, Stanford University Press, Stanford, 2011, translated by Matteo Mandarini; and on the limits of the notion of 'oikos', see Emanuele Coccia, 'Nature is not your household', in Bruno Latour and Peter Weibel (eds), *Critical Zones*, op. cit., pp. 300–4.

The distance introduced between calculation of self-interest and Darwinism is particularly broad with the notion of sequential feature selection; see Ford Doolittle, 'Darwinizing Gaia', *Journal of Theoretical Biology*, 434, 2017: 11–19, and his article, 'Is the Earth an organism?', *Aeon*, December 2020. See also the argument put forward by Timothy Lenton et al., 'Selection for Gaia across multiple scales', *Science Direct*, 33, 8, 2018: 633–45.

8.

Chapter 8, 'Describing a territory – only, the right way round', is based on the experiment of the 'Où atterrir?' consortium this book is dedicated to in the original French version, ouatterrir.fr/index.php/ consortium, an experiment that will be the subject of separate publications. The web version was triggered by the article, 'Inventer les gestes barrières contre le retour à la production d'avant-crise' (Inventing preventive measures against the return to pre-crisis production), in *AOC media*, 29 March 2020, a questionnaire that sparked numerous comments on the internet. But I derive the self-description experiment from the long-term pilot project. On the notion of territory I also take inspiration from Vinciane Despret, *Habiter en oiseau*, Actes Sud, Arles, 2019.

Once again, it's really important not to confuse Gaia with an organism, a theme I developed in 'Why Gaia is not a God of totality', *Theory, Culture and Society*, 34, 2–3, 2017: 61–82.

The notion of 'commons' is enjoying a real comeback. I don't know a better way of overviewing this domain than the remarkable endeavour of Marie Cornu, Fabienne Orsi and Judith Rochfeld, *Dictionnaire des biens communs*, PUF, Paris, 2018.

9.

Like the preceding chapter, Chapter 9, 'The unfreezing of the landscape', turns first to the experiment of the 'Où atterrir?' consortium. The term 'compass' sums up a protocol invented collectively with participants in several French towns and is based on a device developed by the consortium coordinators.

The book by Bruno Latour and Peter Weibel (eds), *Critical Zones*, op. cit., in its content as much as in its form, tries to sum up in much greater detail this general move towards a 'thawing'.

To account for the turnaround imposed by the 'lockdown', I wheel in art history as mobilised in Bruno Latour and Christophe Leclercq (eds), *Reset Modernity!*, MIT Press, Cambridge, Mass., 2016, and of course my book, *We Have Never Been Modern*, Harvard University Press, Cambridge, Mass., 1993, translated by Catherine Porter.

A little further reading

The invention of naturalism is the subject of the book by Philippe Descola, *Beyond Nature and Culture*, University of Chicago Press, Chicago, 2014, translated by Janet Lloyd (originally published 2005), a project he is pursuing in a new, as yet unpublished, book, *Les Formes du visible. Une anthropologie de la figuration*, foreshadowed in *La Fabrique des images*, Editions du Quai Branly-Somogy, Paris, 2010. Frédérique Aït-Touati's work-in-progress on the invention of the landscape scene is presented in part in *Terra Forma*, op. cit. And lastly, see my booklet, *What is the Style of Matters of Concern? Two Lectures in Empirical Philosophy*, Spinoza Lectures, Royal Van Gorcum, Assen, 2008.

The idea of the reversal of ownership is argued by Sarah Vanuxem in *La Propriété de la terre*, Wild Project, Marseilles, 2018, and in 'Freedom from easements', in Bruno Latour and Peter Weibel (eds), *Critical Zones*, op. cit., pp. 240–7. On the reversal of the common landscape in anthropology, see Deborah Bird Rose, *Wild Dog Dreaming: Love and Extinction*, University of Virginia Press, Charlottesville, 2011. See also the beautiful catalogue edited by Juliette Dumasy-Rabineau, Nadine Gastaldi and Camille Serchuk, *Quand les artistes dessinaient les cartes. Vues et figures de l'espace français, Moyen Age et Renaissance*, Archives nationales and Editions Le Passage, Paris, 2019.

The reversal of the relationship between the individual and society is at the heart of the actor-network. See my *Reassembling the Social: An Introduction to Actor-Network-Theory*, Oxford University Press, Oxford, 2005.

A little further reading

10

In Chapter 10, 'Mortal bodies are piling up', I take a sidelong glance at STS (science–technology–society) literature, in particular the fascinating book by Anne-Marie Moil, *The Body Multiple: Ontology in Medical Practice*, Duke University Press, Durham and London, 2003; as well as Ivan Illich's classic, *Medical Nemesis: The Expropriation of Health*, 1975, and especially his sadly little-known work, *Gender*, Pantheon Books, New York, 1982. On capturing the body, see Evelyn Fox-Keller, *Keywords in Evolutionary Biology* (co-edited with Elisabeth Lloyd), Harvard University Press, 1998 (first published 1992), as well as my article, 'How to talk about the body? The normative dimension of science studies', *Body and Society*, 10, 2/3, 2004: 205–29. On the proliferation of the capturing of the suffering body, see Tobie Nathan and Isabelle Stengers, *Doctors and Healers*, Polity, Cambridge, 2018 (originally *Médecins et sorciers*, La Découverte, collection 'Les Empêcheurs de penser en rond', Paris, 1995).

The idea of the reversal of inside–outside relationships owes much to Raymond Ruyer, *Néo-finalisme*, PUF, 2013 (1952) and the continuity of the experiment, of course, to William James. On this tradition, see Isabelle Stengers, *Réactiver le sens commun*, La Découverte, collection 'Les Empêcheurs de penser en rond', Paris, 2020. To my mind, Donna Haraway has gone further than anyone in the merging of various feminisms and biologies, from Laurence Allard, Delphine Gardey and Nathalie Magnan (eds), *Manifeste cyborg et autres essais*, Exils éditeur, Paris, 2007, to *Vivre avec le trouble*, op. cit. See Emilie Hache's work-in-progress,

'Né-e-s de la terre. Un nouveau mythe pour les terres-tres', loc. cit.

11.

Chapter 11, 'The return of ethnogeneses', takes up my dramatisation of the planets, "We don't seem to live on the same planet', in Bruno Latour and Peter Weibel (eds), *Critical Zones*, op. cit., pp. 276–82, as well as the article with Dipesh Chakrabarty, 'Conflicts of planetary proportions: a conversation', *Journal of the Philosophy of History*, 14, 3, 2020: 419–54. I pursue this issue with Martin Guinard in the Taipei Biennale of Art exhibition, *You and I Don't Live on the Same Planet*, 2020–2021.

As for 'regimes of planetarity', these derive from Christophe Bonneuil, *L'Historien et la Planète. Penser les régimes de planétarité à la croisée des écologies-monde, des réflexivités environnementales et des géopouvoirs* (to be published). For the planet Exit, I draw on Nikolaj Schultz, 'Life as Exodus', in Bruno Latour and Peter Weibel (eds), *Critical Zones*, op. cit., pp. 284–8, followed by Nastassja Martin, *Les Ames sauvages. Face à l'Occident, la résistance d'un peuple d'Alaska*, La Découverte, Paris, 2016.

On the key notion of diplomacy, see Isabelle Stengers, *La Vierge et le Neutrino*, Seuil/'Les Empêcheurs de penser en rond', Paris, 2005, as well as 'La proposition cosmopolitique' in Jacques Lolive et Olivier Soubeyran (eds), *L'Emergence des cosmopolitiques*, La Decouverte, Paris, 2007, pp. 45–68. I deeply admire the daily labour pursued by The Decolonial Atlas, decolonialatlas.wordpress.com. On the key notion of encroachment, see Patrice Maniglier, 'Petit traité de

A little further reading

Gaïapolitique', in Frédérique Aït-Touati and Emanuele Coccia (eds), *Le Cri de Gaïa*, op. cit., pp. 185–217.

On the necessity of anthropocentrism, see Clive Hamilton, *Defiant Earth: The Fate of Humans in the Anthropocene*, Polity, Cambridge, 2017. There's a whole body of literature on the Anthropocene, so it's better to go to the source of the data: Jan Zalasiewicz, *The Anthropocene as a Geological Unit*, Cambridge University Press, Cambridge, 2019.

I took the notion of a monad superimposed in many different ways from Gabriel Tarde, *Monadology and Sociology*, re-press, Melbourne, 2012 (1895). For a development of this intuition, see in particular Bruno Latour et al., '"Le tout est toujours plus petit que ses parties". Une expérimentation numérique des monades de Gabriel Tarde', *Réseaux*, 31, 1, 2013: 199–233.

The opposition between royal science and nomadic or ambulatory science is taken from Gilles Deleuze and Félix Guattari, *A Thousand Plateaus: Capitalism and Schizophrenia*, University of Minnesota Press, Minneapolis, 1987 (originally published 1980).

On the variable dimension of Gaia time, once again see Lenton et al., 'Selection for Gaia across multiple scales', loc. cit., and for the impact of the Anthropocene, Timothy Lenton and Bruno Latour, 'Gaia 2.0', *Science*, 14 September 2018: 1066–8.

12.

In Chapter 12, 'Some pretty strange battles', I again draw on Pierre Charbonnier, *Abondance et liberté*, op. cit., and on Nikolaj Schultz's work on the geo-social classes, in particular 'New climates, new class struggles', in Bruno Latour and Peter Weibel (eds), *Critical Zones*, op. cit., pp. 308–12. A portrait of the Extractors is drawn in the works of Saskia Sassen, in particular *Expulsions: Brutality and Complexity in the Global Economy*, Belknap Press, Cambridge, Mass., 2014. See also Luca Chancel, *Insoutenables inégalités*, Les petits matins, Paris, 2017.

13.

In Chapter 13, 'Scattering in all directions', I use the abacus invented by the Global Footprint Network. On the moving of the lockdown date over the northern spring of 2020, see futura-sciences.com/ planete/ actualites/developpement-durable-jour-depassement-recul-exceptionnel-trois-semaines-63853/.

On the startling insertion of the invisible theory of self-regulation in climate negotiations, see Stefan Aykut and Amy Dahan, *Gouverner le climat? Vingt ans de négociation climatique*, Presses de Sciences Po, Paris, 2015, and the detailed analysis of Lovelock's influence on earth system science, in Sébastien Dutreuil, *Gaïa. Hypothèse, programme de recherche pour le système terre, ou philosophie de la nature?*, op. cit. The term self-regulation is the actual subject of the tension between Lovelock, who leans towards a cybernetic model, and Margulis, who works with living beings step by step without a global model.

For ten years I've been pursuing theatre experiments with Frédérique Aït-Touati, aimed at staging the scientific concept of Gaia literally, against the usual cosmological evidence. See the different recordings on *Inside*, 2018, *Moving Earths*, 2019: youtube.com/watch

?v=ANhumN6INfI&feature=youtube; and the play *Gaia Global Circus*, text by Pierre Daubigny.

The link between the issue of the state and new forms of Gaia's sovereignty is the subject of my last three lectures in *Facing Gaia*, op. cit., pp. 239–73. I draw on Dorothea and Pierre-Yves Condé's ongoing research.

To understand the opposition between Gaia and the notion of the globe or of globality, see my article, 'Why Gaia is not a God of totality', loc. cit. The notion of the nomos of the earth derives, of course, from the decisive book by Carl Schmitt, *The Nomos of the Earth in the International Law of the Jus Publicum*, Telos Press, Candor N.Y., 2003 (first published 1950). On the new notion of space implied by Schmitt, see my 'How to remain human in the wrong space? A comment on a dialog by Carl Schmitt', *Critical Enquiry*, to be published.

On the anthropology of various earth and fertility cults, see the fascinating anthology edited by Renée Koch-Piettre, Odile Journet and Danouta Liberski-Bagnoud, *Mémoires de la Terre. Etudes anciennes et comparées*, Jérôme Millon, Grenoble, 2020. Iliich's injunction is from his book *The Corruption of Christianity*, op. cit.